ABANDONED MARYLAND HOUSES

RUINS OF THE AMERICAN DREAM

ROBYN AND RHEA HODGSON

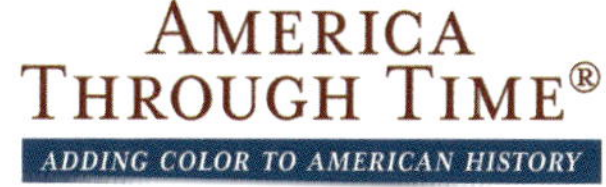

We dedicate this book to those Maryland explorers we respect and admire. You know who you are. We dedicate this book to our grandchildren. May you view the corners of the world with vivid curiosity. Finally, we dedicate this book to each other. Through our photography and backroad adventures, we have forged a deeper relationship, friendship, and marriage.

America Through Time is an imprint of Fonthill Media LLC
www.through-time.com
office@through-time.com

Published by Arcadia Publishing by arrangement with Fonthill Media LLC
For all general information, please contact Arcadia Publishing:
Telephone: 843-853-2070
Fax: 843-853-0044
E-mail: sales@arcadiapublishing.com
For customer service and orders:
Toll-Free 1-888-313-2665

www.arcadiapublishing.com

First published 2022

ISBN 978-1-63499-436-1

Typeset in 10pt on 13pt Trade Gothic
Printed and bound in England

CONTENTS

ABOUT THE AUTHORS

Robyn and Rhea have been together and in love for more than twenty years. (Rhea came out as transgender in February 2022.) They have four children and five grandchildren. Robyn, a former journalist, is a writing tutor and adjunct writing instructor of at-risk college students, and Rhea is an occupational therapy practitioner in a nursing rehab facility. Both share a passion for history and photography and traveling the backroads exploring historic locations. They believe that each house contains a story and a memory. Their hope is that many of the homes they discover can be saved from the wrecking ball.

INTRODUCTION

When one thinks of abandoned houses in Maryland, one often contemplates the mass dereliction affecting the city of Baltimore where there are at least 16,000 abandoned homes. While this book recognizes the plight of the inner city, its focus centers on photos of rural and suburban blight that often remains overlooked. Across Maryland, there are thousands of vacant and abandoned houses, many hidden behind overgrown trees and tucked in tiny towns far from the busy metro centers. Many of these homes possess rich histories, ties to former settlers who forged the path to what the state is today. That history is reflected from the Colonial Era, African American settlements, the boom of the Industrial Revolution through the Gilded Age, and its vast agricultural farmland. The land dictates the homes, too, as the landscape and topography fluctuate from the salt-rich marsh of the Eastern Shore to the plateaus, and the Appalachian region of the western pinnacle.

We want our readers to know that each abandoned home has a unique story, often underscored by heartache and misfortune. We want to give the reader a new understanding, so that when they see a dilapidated house they might respond with a deeper level of empathy and a sense of historical reference. Understand, however, we are withholding revealing details that may betray the locations of certain homes still standing, because it is our hope that these ruins can undergo renovation and restoration and not fall victim to vandalism and further neglect.

1

MARYLAND'S HISTORY

In order to understand the architecture and the lost homes that dot the landscape, we feel it is crucial to learn about the colonists' roots who traveled to the land of what would transform into Maryland, and what would evolve into a haven for Catholics, convicts, and indentured servants. It began when King Charles I granted the 2nd Baron of Baltimore, Cecilus Calvert, the charter for the colony after the 1st Baron of Baltimore had died. They would then name the colony after the king's wife, Queen Henrietta Maria.

The Baron's younger brother Leonard Calvert set sail for Maryland on two ships named the *Ark* and the *Dove*, arriving in 1634 on St. Clement's Island in southern Maryland. The first colonists included less than twenty gentry, their wives, and 200 indentured servants who could work off their passage. They bought land from the Yaocomico Indians—paying them with ordinary items carried on the ships such as garden hoes, hatchets, beads, and mirrors—and established the town of St. Mary's on the Chesapeake Bay.

Religious persecution in England would send Catholics fleeing to Maryland. Religious turmoil would continue to percolate within Maryland as its nature would transform from Catholic to Anglicism and then again once the Puritans took hold in 1650. A battle occurred between Lord Baltimore's Catholic army and the Puritans with the latter defeating the former in the Battle of the Severn. Puritans severely persecuted Catholics by burning all the original Catholic churches. In 1658, the Calvert family seized back control of Maryland and passed the Toleration Act.

In the early 1700s, the governmental seat was moved to Providence and was renamed Annapolis after Queen Anne. The city's plan was laid out to symbolize a strong tie between the colonial government and the Protestant church.

The colony evolved into a rich source of income through tobacco crops—as slave labor toiled on plantations. The Crown sentenced convicts to transportation terms in Maryland, which ceased at the conclusion of the Revolutionary War. To solve a boundary dispute between Pennsylvania and Maryland, in 1750, surveyors, Charles Mason and Jeremiah Dixon, established the boundary known as the Mason–Dixon Line, which became the demarcation between the slave-holding states and the Union before the Civil War. Although Maryland allowed slavery, the state did not secede from the Union. Nonetheless, many residents remained sympathetic to the Confederacy.

2

LOST FARMS: AMERICA'S HEART

Sprinkled throughout Maryland, tree-lined paths and overgrowth conceal thousands of vacant and abandoned homes and farmhouses. These houses wait for someone to save them from demolition by developers, because urban and suburban sprawl remains the largest threat to farms, which are often historic structures. Demolishing historic farms and houses transforms the character of pastoral communities and turns them into cookie-cutter neighborhoods. In fact, the United States is losing "175 acres per hour" of farmland, according to the Montgomery Countryside Alliance, a farmland protection advocacy group. For example, development has stripped Harford and Frederick counties of much of its bucolic scenery, 30% and 15%, between 1997 and 2012, respectively, a 2017 article in the *Capital News Service* reports.

Selling to a developer is not always the first step. The reasons farmers and homeowners abandon their home vary, but they almost always involve misfortune and loss. Abandonment can happen when properties are transferred to the banks, home foreclosures, unpaid taxes, eminent domain, and the sometimes long process of estate auctions. The truth is, no one buys a house expecting to let it be reclaimed by nature, vandals, or drug addicts. Declining industries, restrictive housing and finance policies, harsh code enforcement, or personal tragedies can become intertwined into the story of a disembodied home.

For many farmers, high supply prices push them out of business. Others may quit due to rising medical bills, signing their home over to the state to qualify for Medicaid healthcare, so they can afford long-term care in a nursing home. Once they do, the states cannot sell the house until the owner has died, and the estate finishes the probate process. As a result, while grandma languishes in a facility with dementia, her home is subject to vandalism, theft, and the elements.

In addition to the before mentioned, the environment plays a role in families deserting a home such as natural disasters and climate change. For example, saltwater is infiltrating the soil on the Eastern Shore of Maryland, where many of the state's oldest domiciles remain.

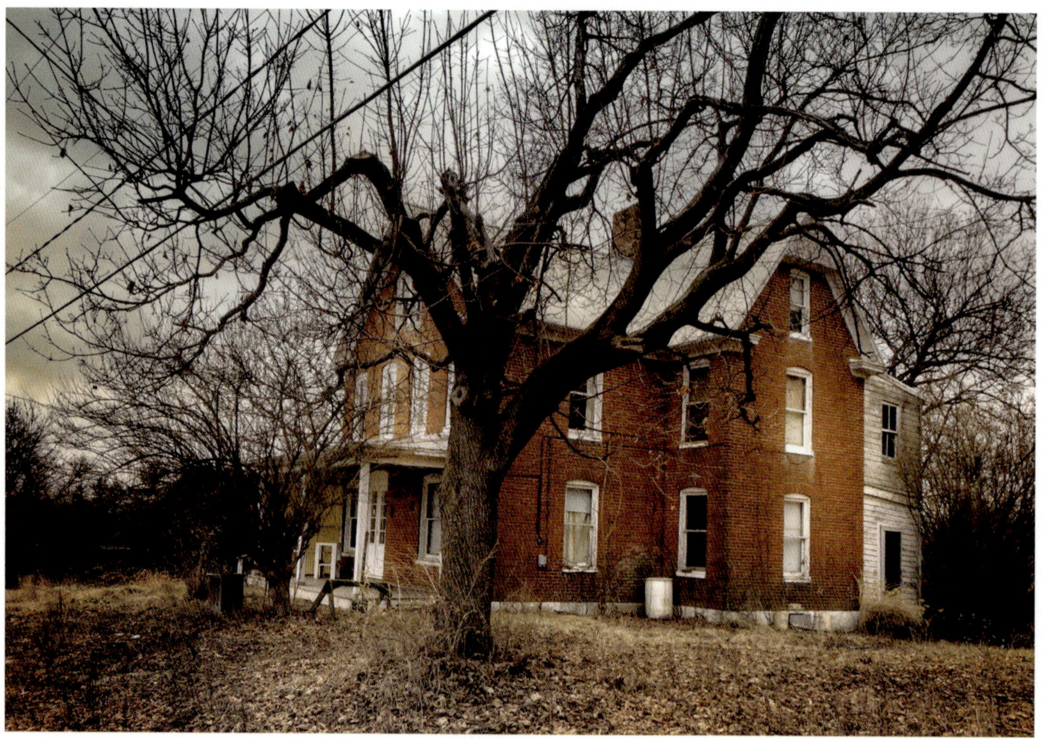

A two-story brick Victorian now owned by the state of Maryland. [*Robyn*].

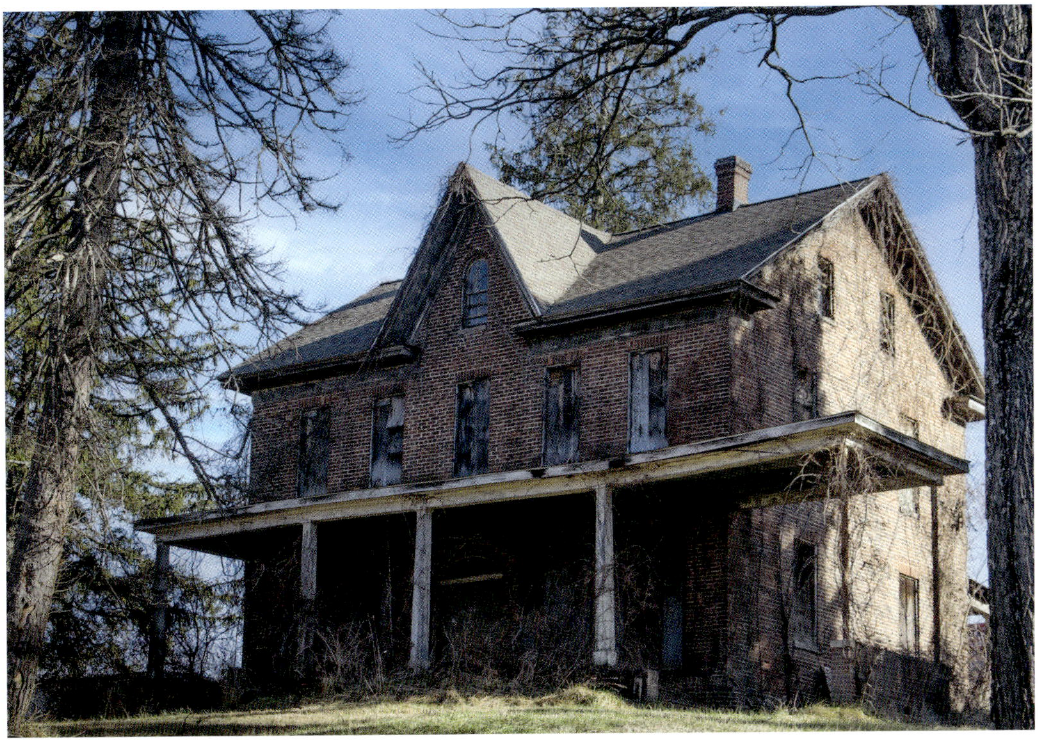

A dilapidated farmhouse in the Baltimore area. [*Rhea*]

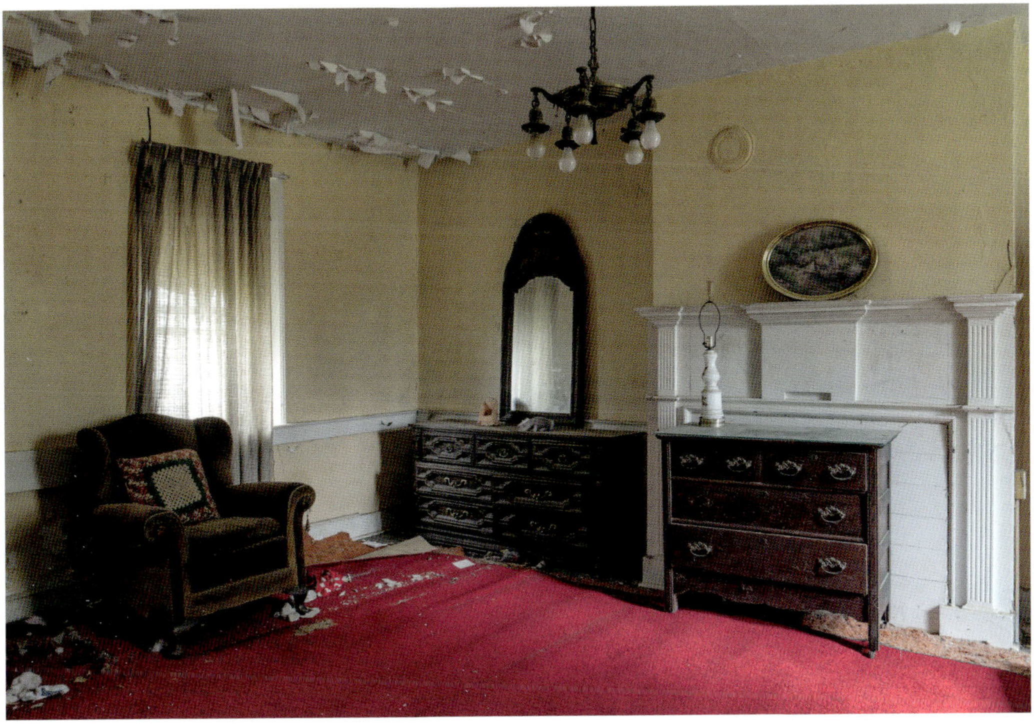

Left to time, cobwebs filled this farm. [*Robyn*]

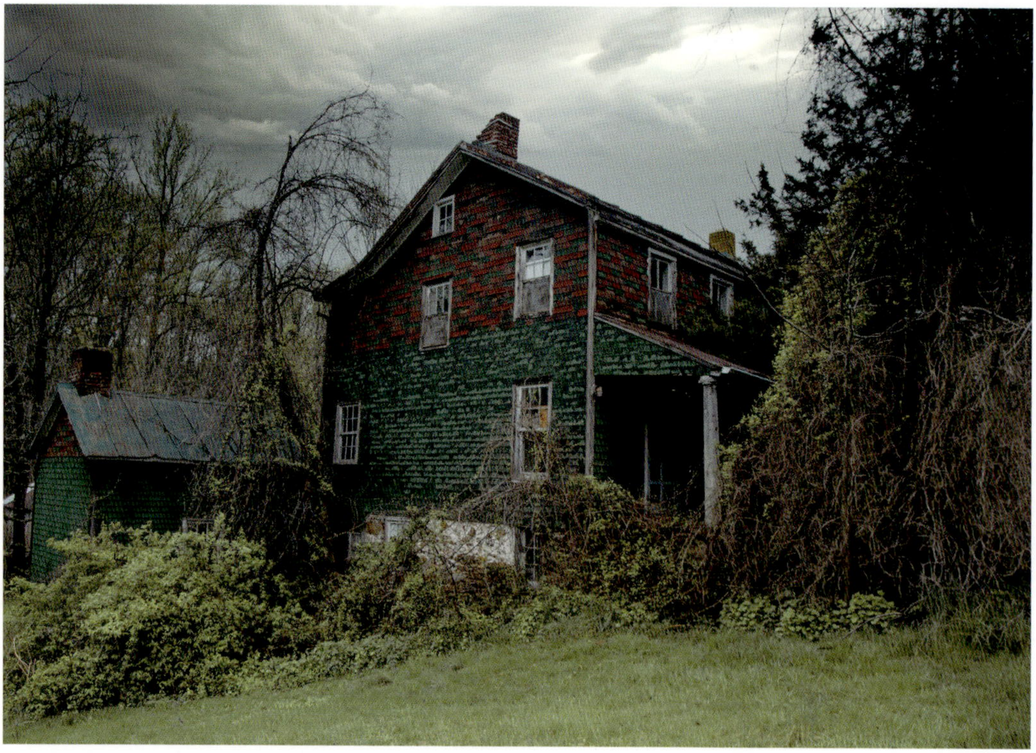

An abandoned farmhouse in the Piedmont Plateau. [*Robyn*]

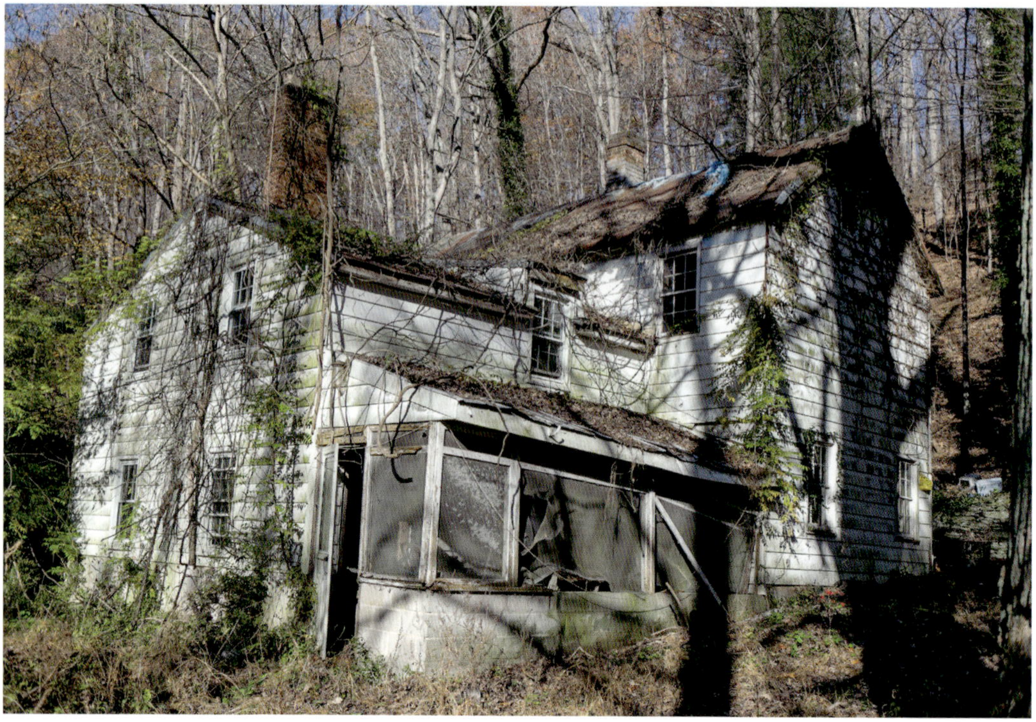

An abandoned farmhouse in the Piedmont Plateau. [*Robyn*]

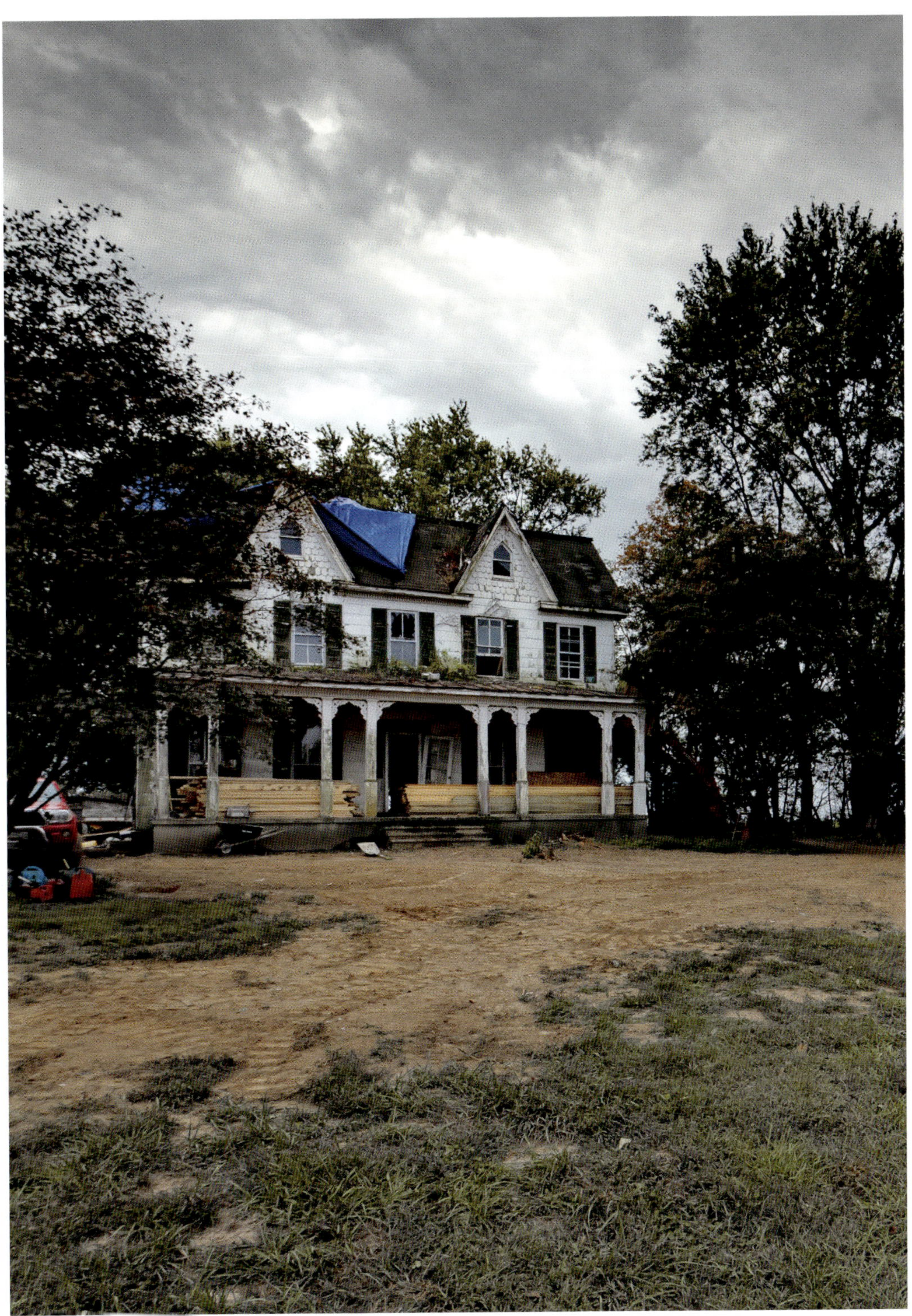

When we first explored this massive farmhouse, antiques, newspapers, magazines, and trash were piled waist-high in every room. Some floors had collapsed. This photo depicts renovations underway. The house has been cleared, and the frame has been rebuilt, proving anything can be salvaged. [*Robyn*]

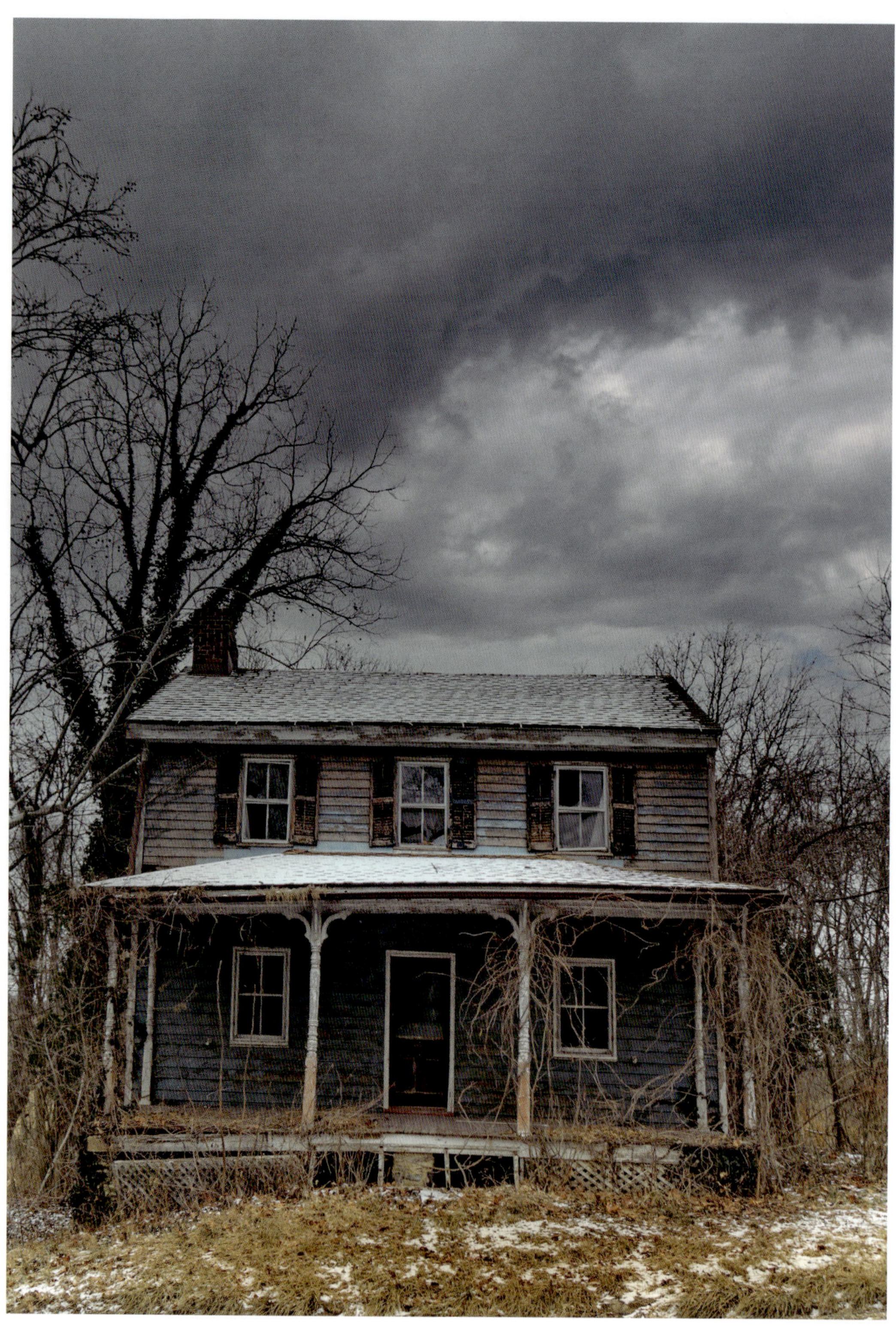

Some explorers have dubbed this house the "murder farm" because someone had taped photos of missing children on the wall. [*Robyn*]

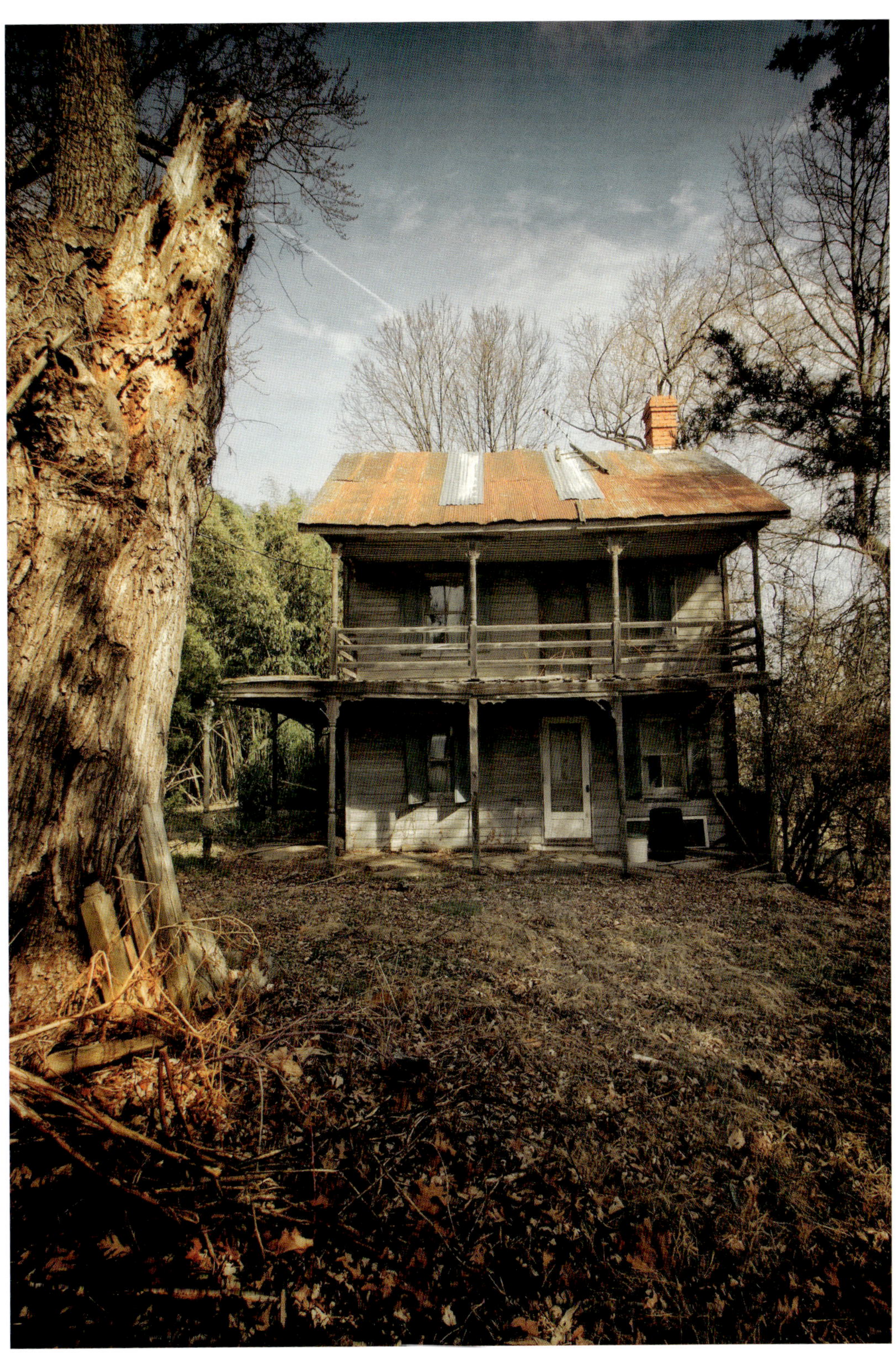

An abandoned house in southern Maryland. [*Robyn*]

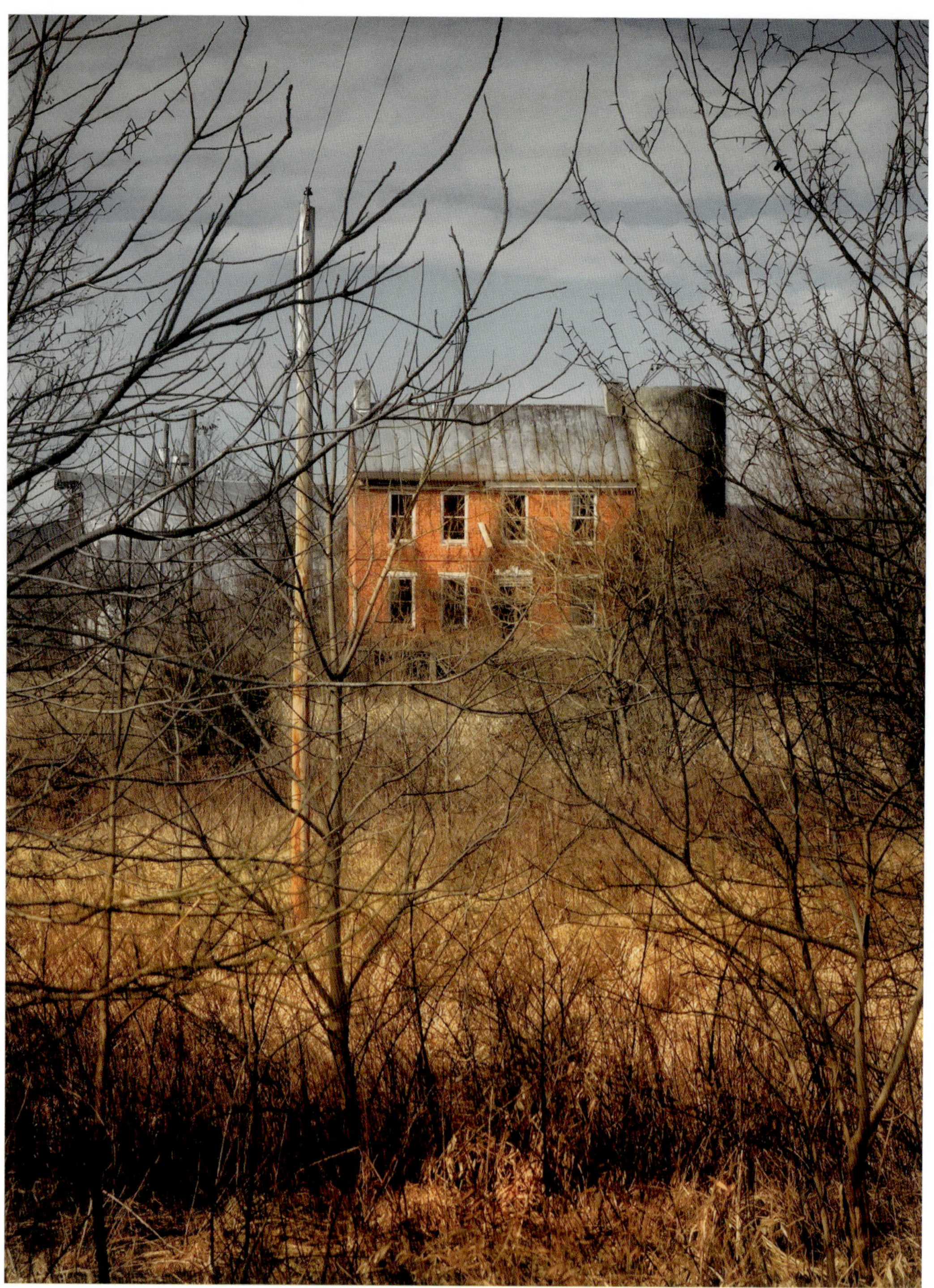

A more than 200-year-old farm in the plateau region. [*Rhea*]

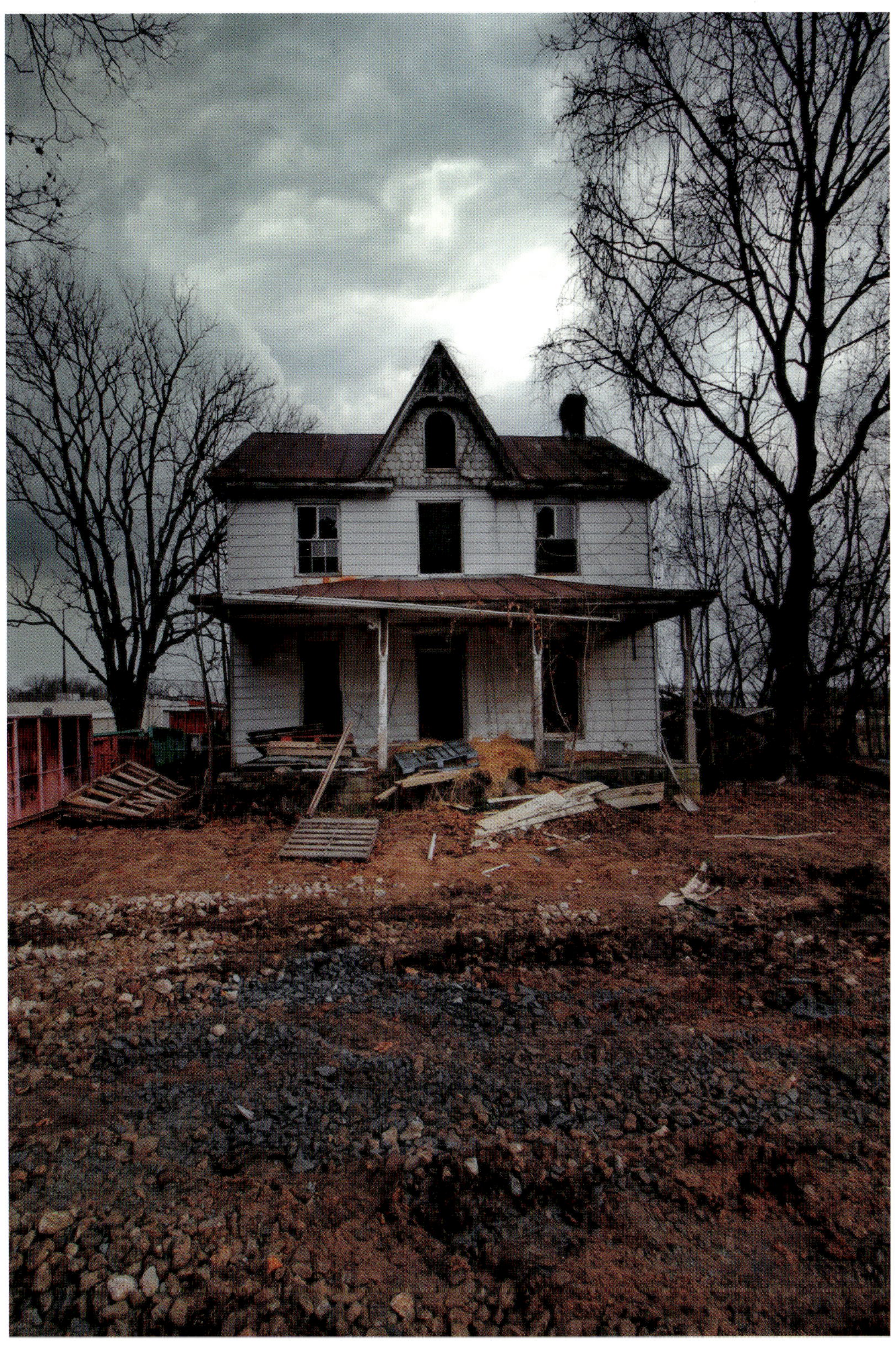

A Folk Victorian house in the process of demolition. [*Robyn*]

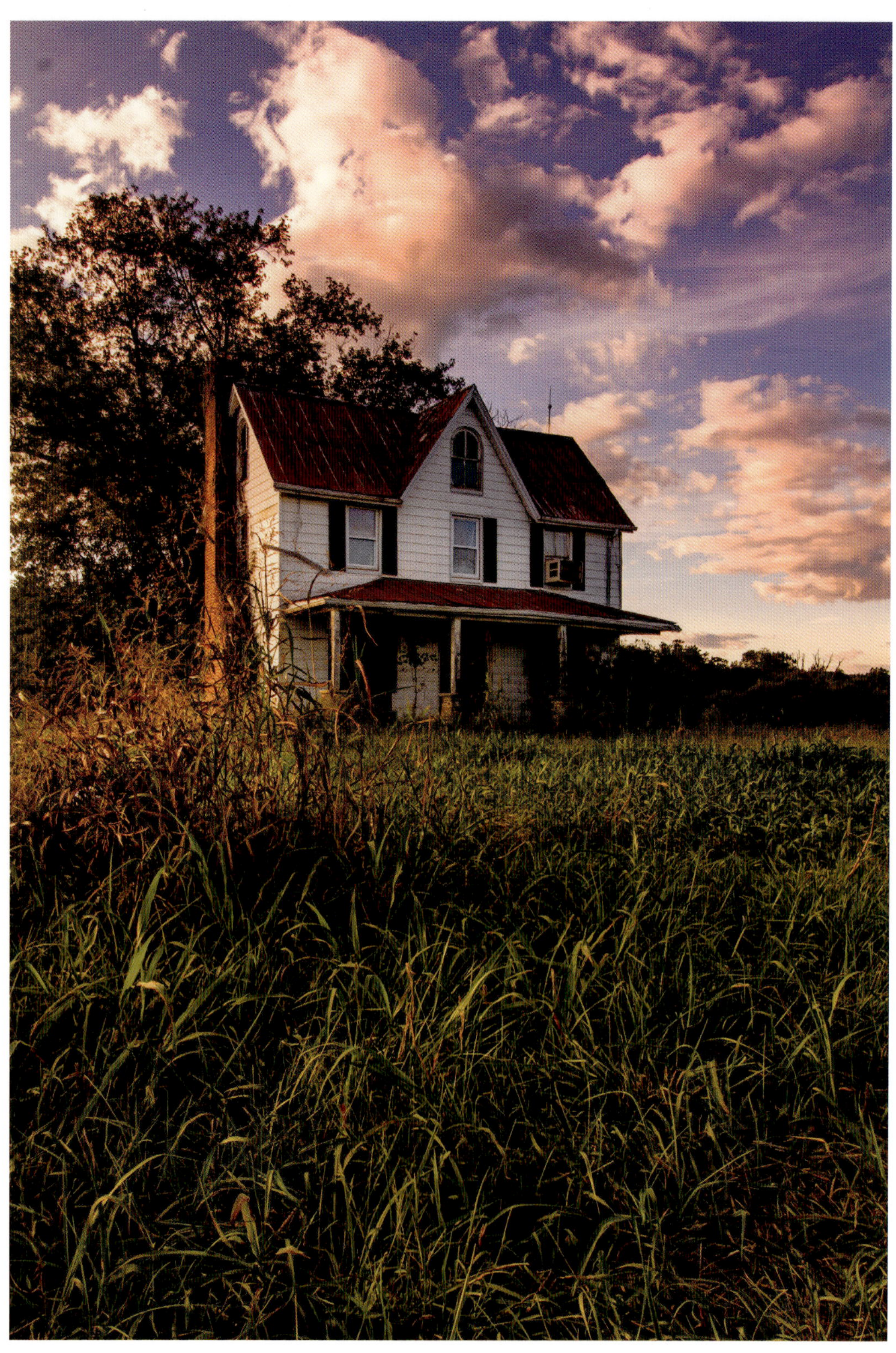

A Victorian farm sits lonely in a field amid modern development. [*Robyn*]

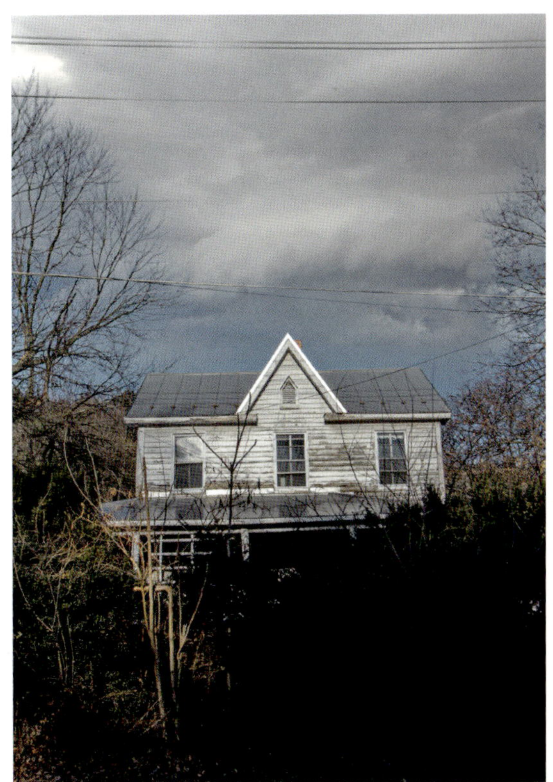

A Victorian farmhouse in the Piedmont Plateau region that is being renovated by the ancestral family. [*Robyn*]

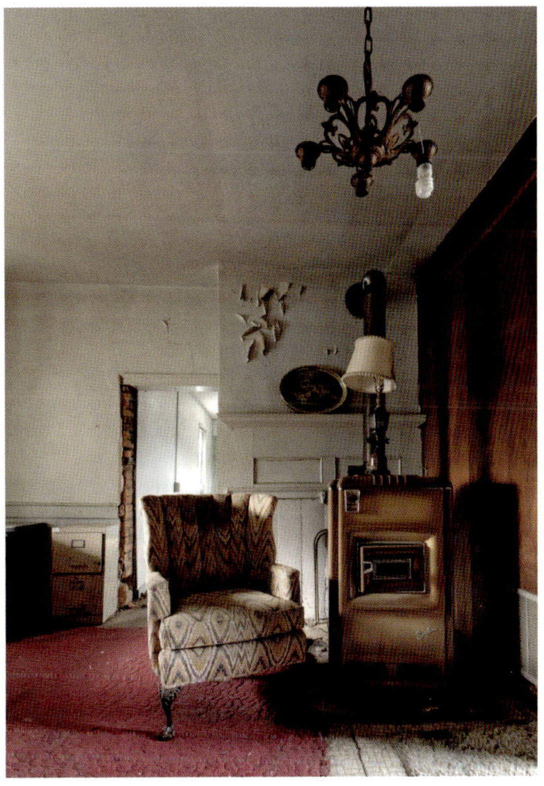

An early twentieth-century chair and light fixture remain in a plateau region farm. [*Robyn*]

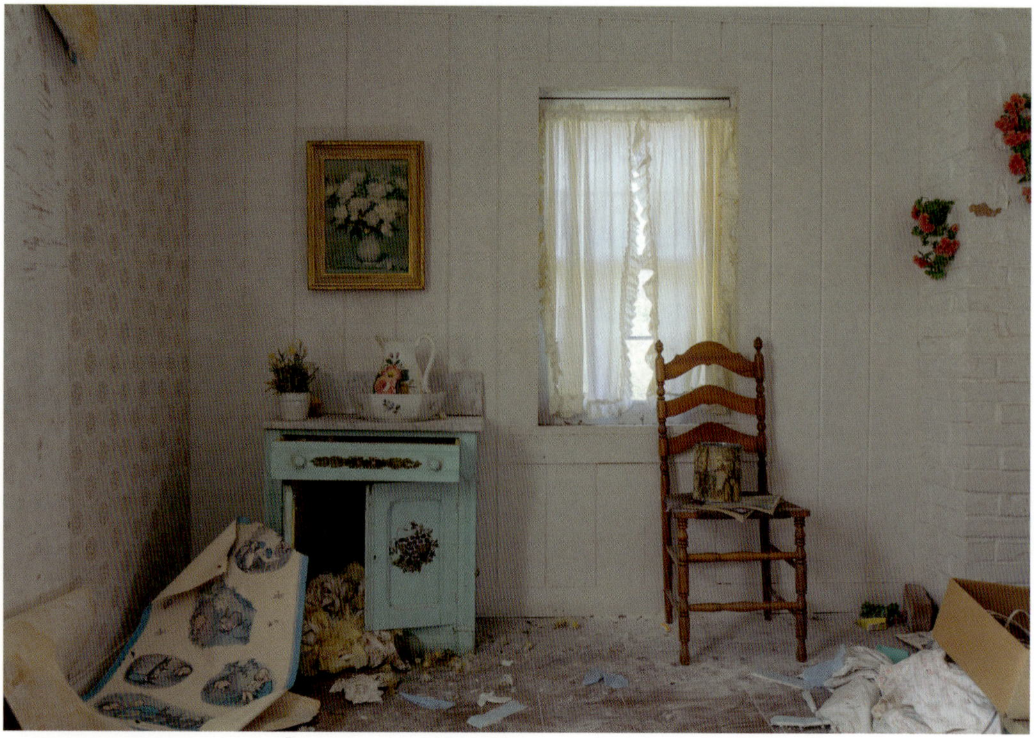

An antique wash pitcher and stand in an abandoned plateau area farm that was built in 1900. [*Rhea*]

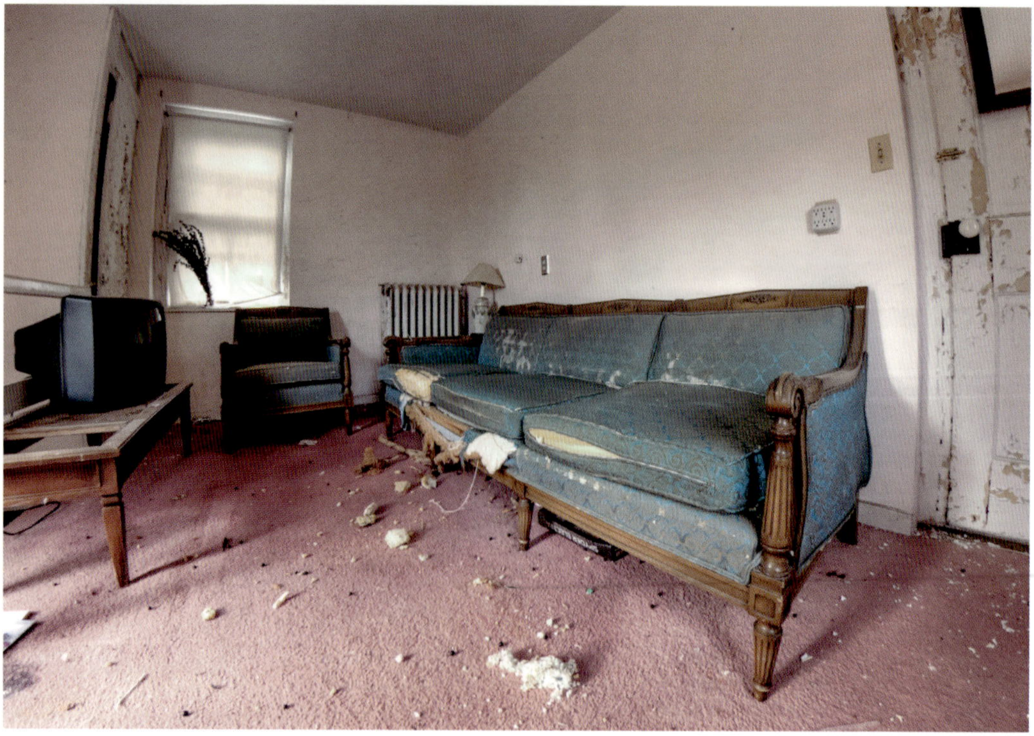

A spare room inside an abandoned Victorian farm that is full of mouse feces. [*Robyn*].

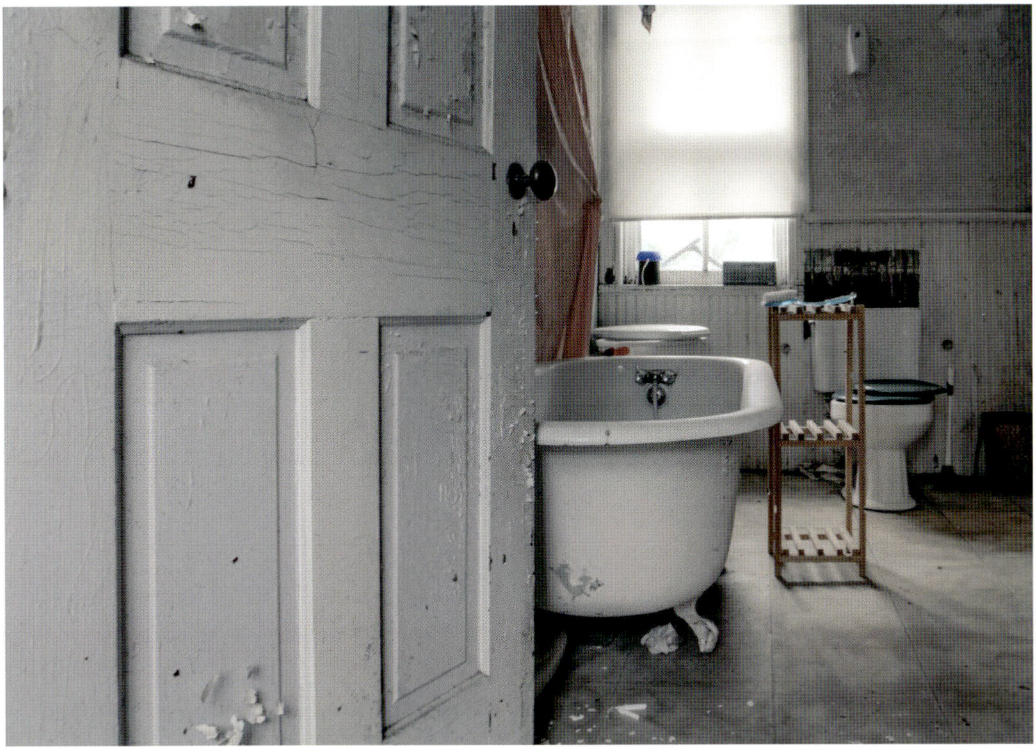

The bear claw tub inside an abandoned Victorian farm photographed four years apart. The house began to sag due to kids vandalizing the windows, allowing water to damage the floors. [*Robyn*]

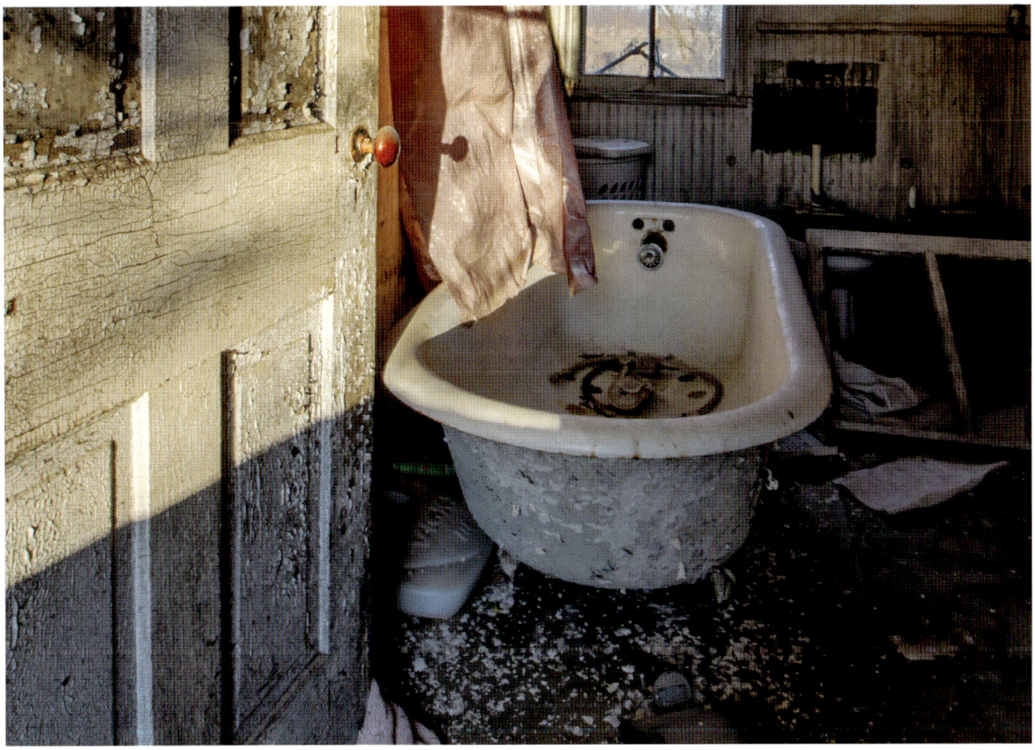

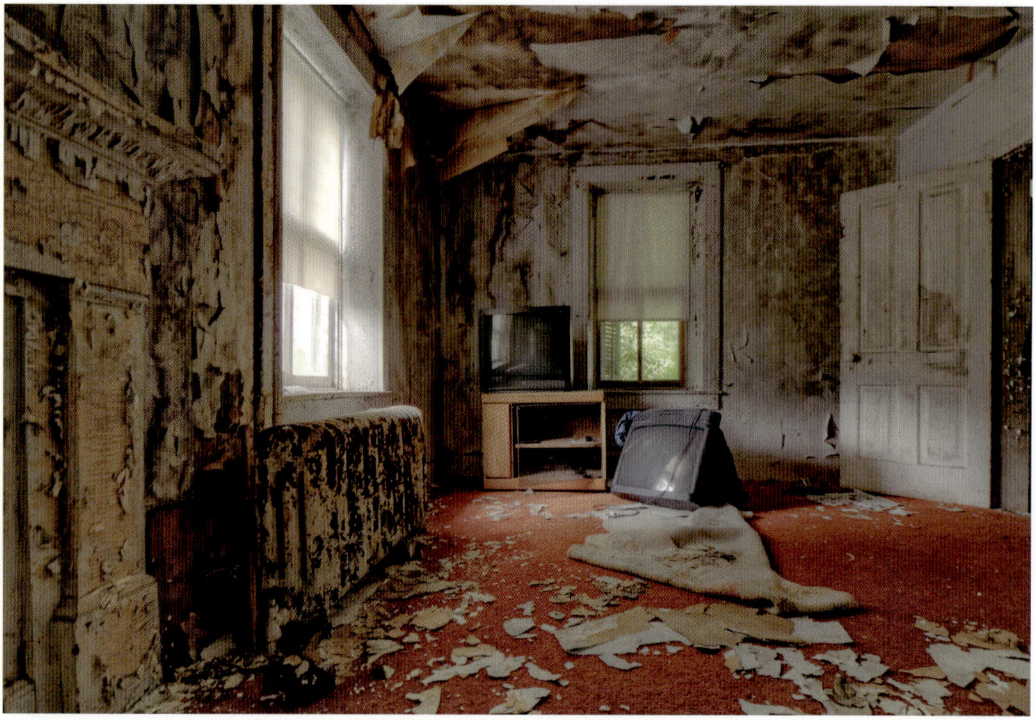

Old TVs sit on a crumbling floor of an abandoned farm. [*Robyn*]

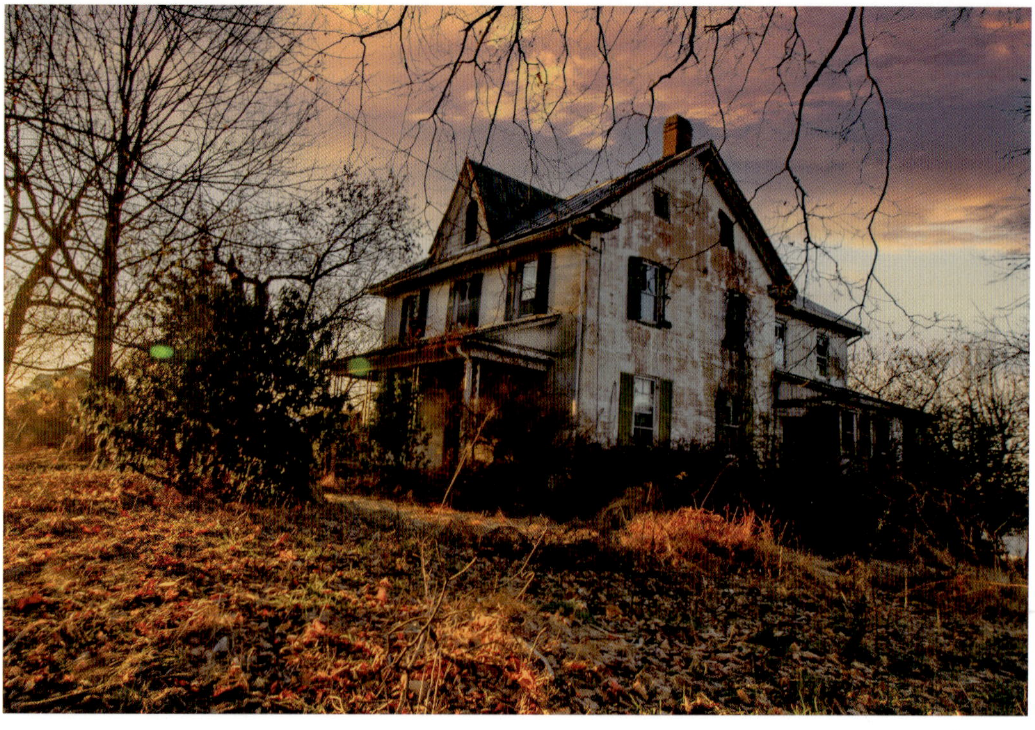

This historic farm is at risk for demolition due to its location. We were unable to discover its history but estimate it is more than 200 years old. [*Rhea*]

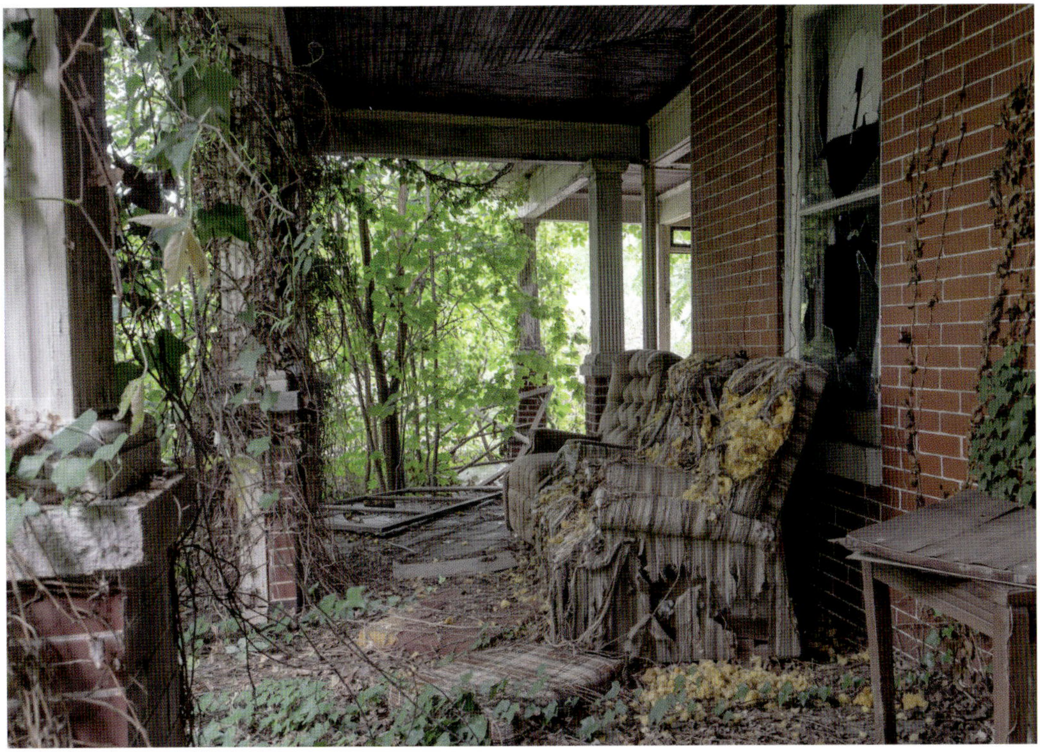

Furniture falls apart on a porch of a Victorian farmhouse in the plateau region. [*Rhea*]

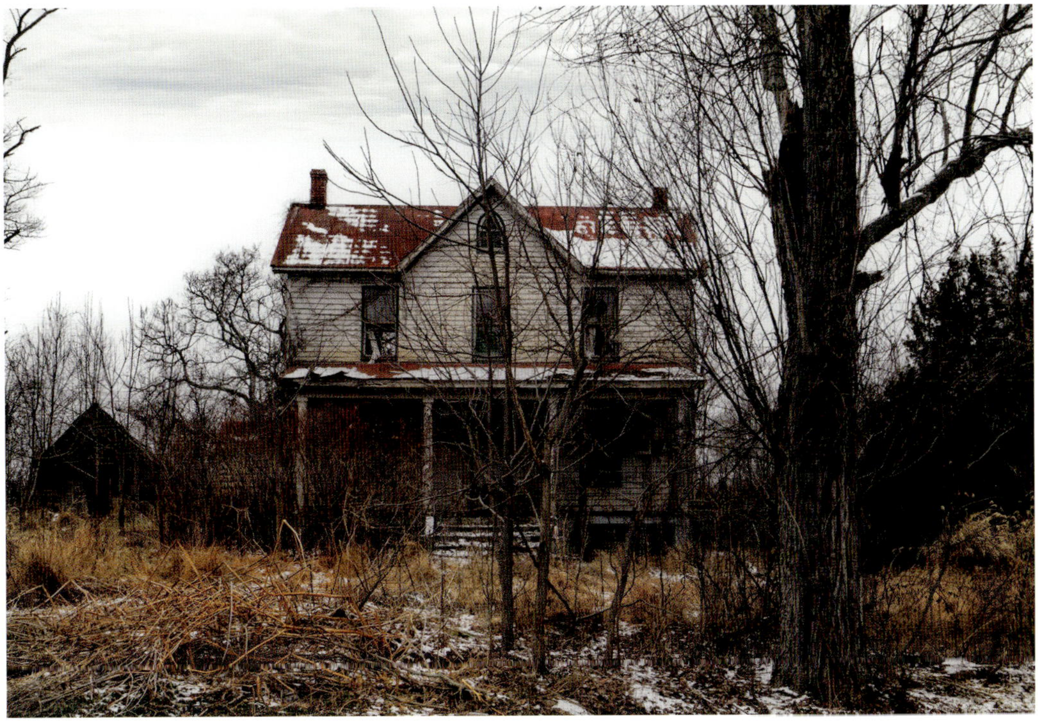

A spooky dilapidated farm that is endangered by development on a wintry day. [*Robyn*]

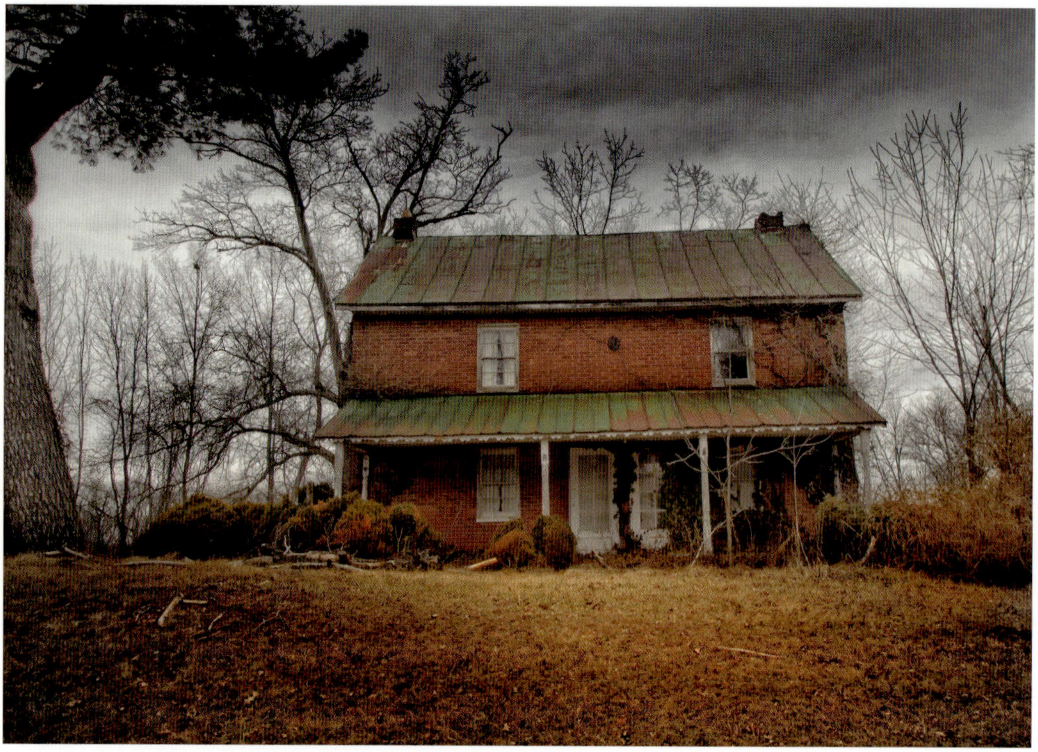

This bungalow was built in the early twentieth century and has no indoor plumbing. [*Robyn*]

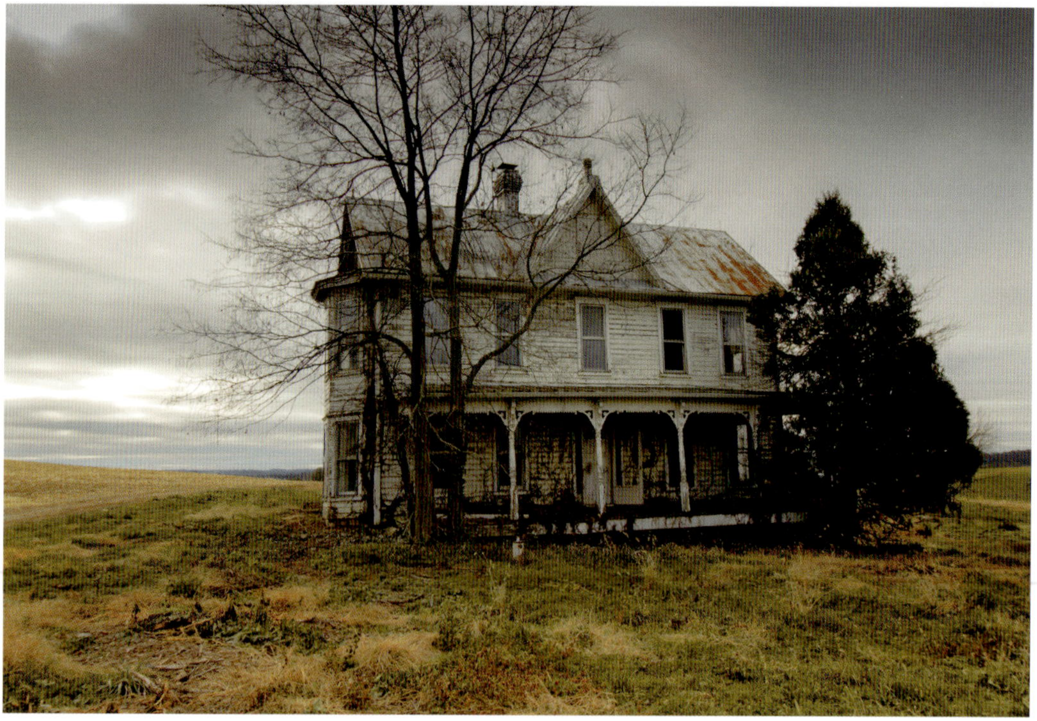

An ornate Folk Victorian farmhouse, likely built in the late 1800s, that is probably destined for demolition. [*Robyn*]

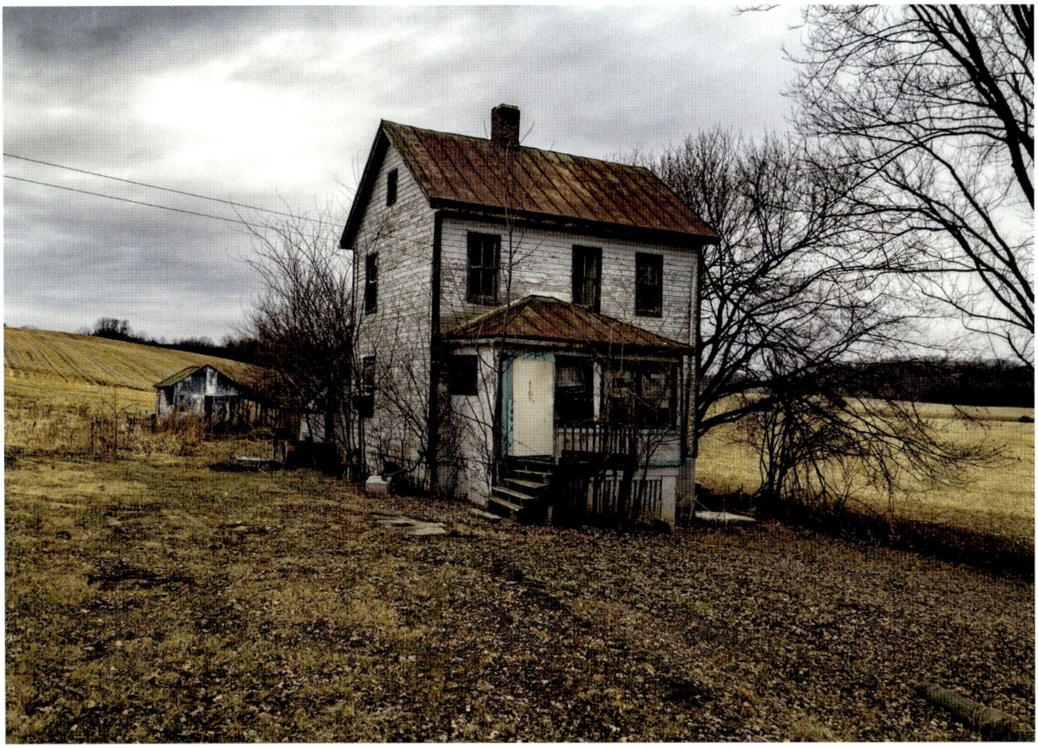

Rumor has it that someone was murdered in this gutted house. [*Robyn*].

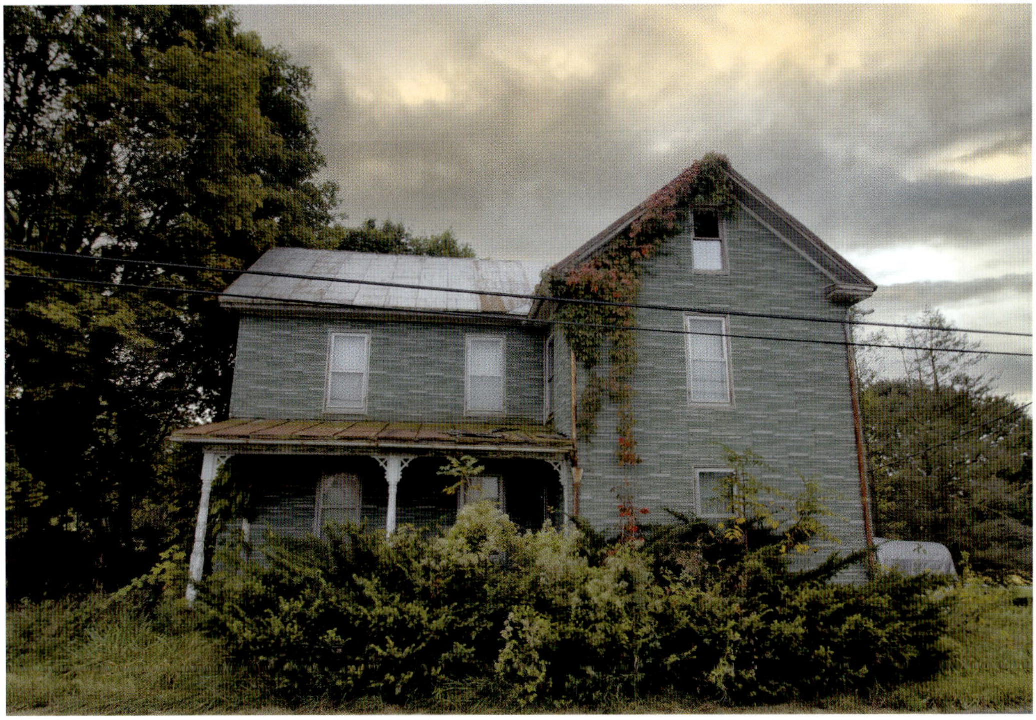

A Victorian farmhouse decays in the plateau region. [*Robyn*]

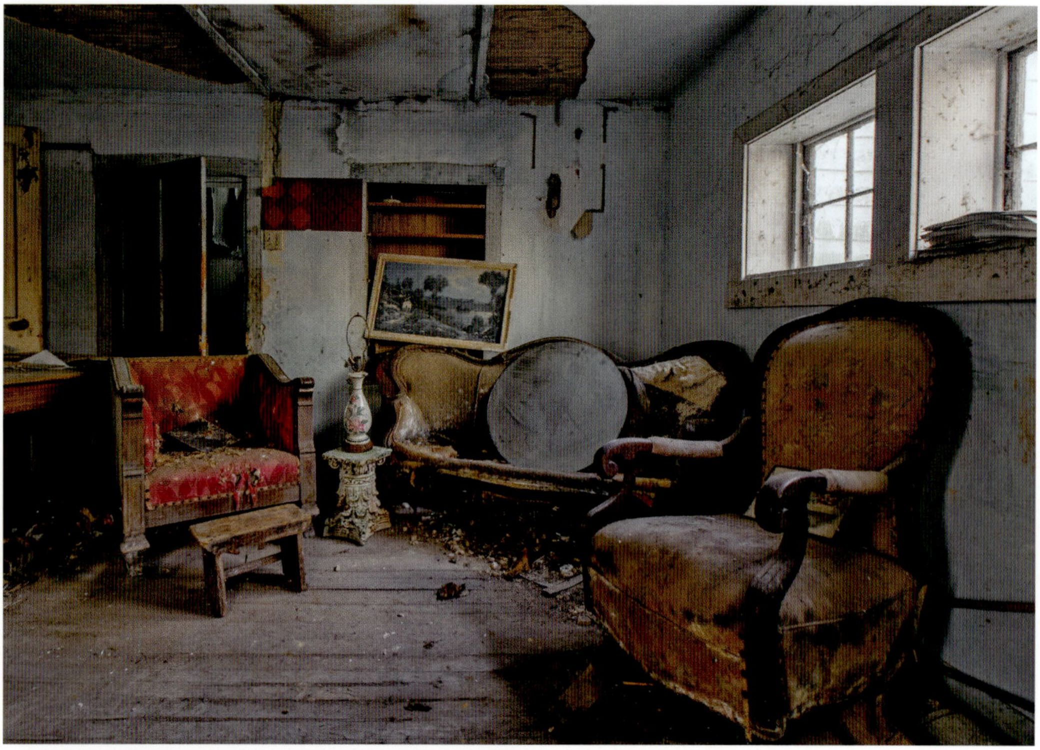

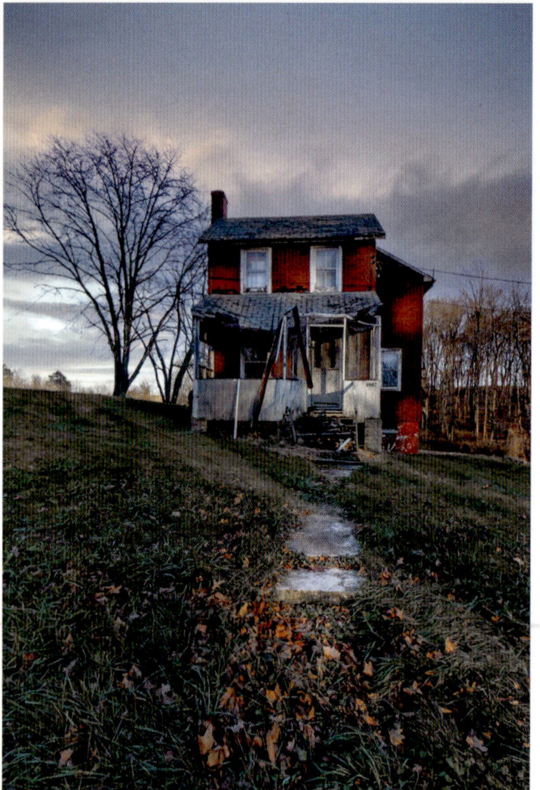

Above: Antiques deteriorate inside a plateau-area farmhouse. [*Rhea*]

Left: An early twentieth-century home that bears ugly carpet. [*Robyn*]

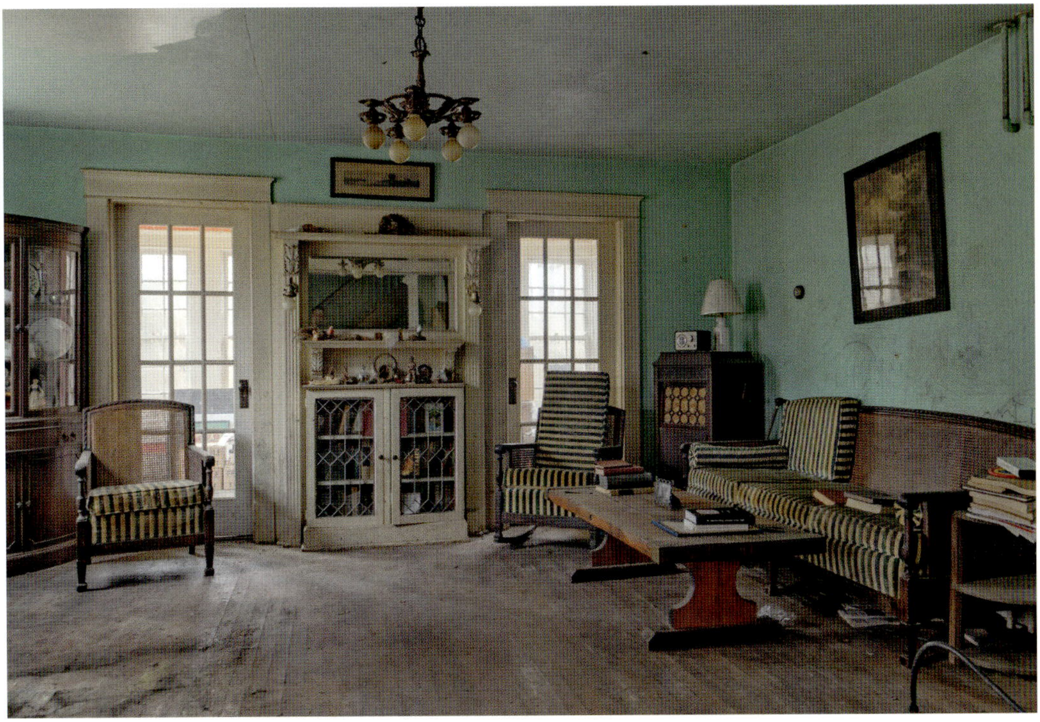

Vintage furniture rots in a 200-year-old manor. [*Rhea*]

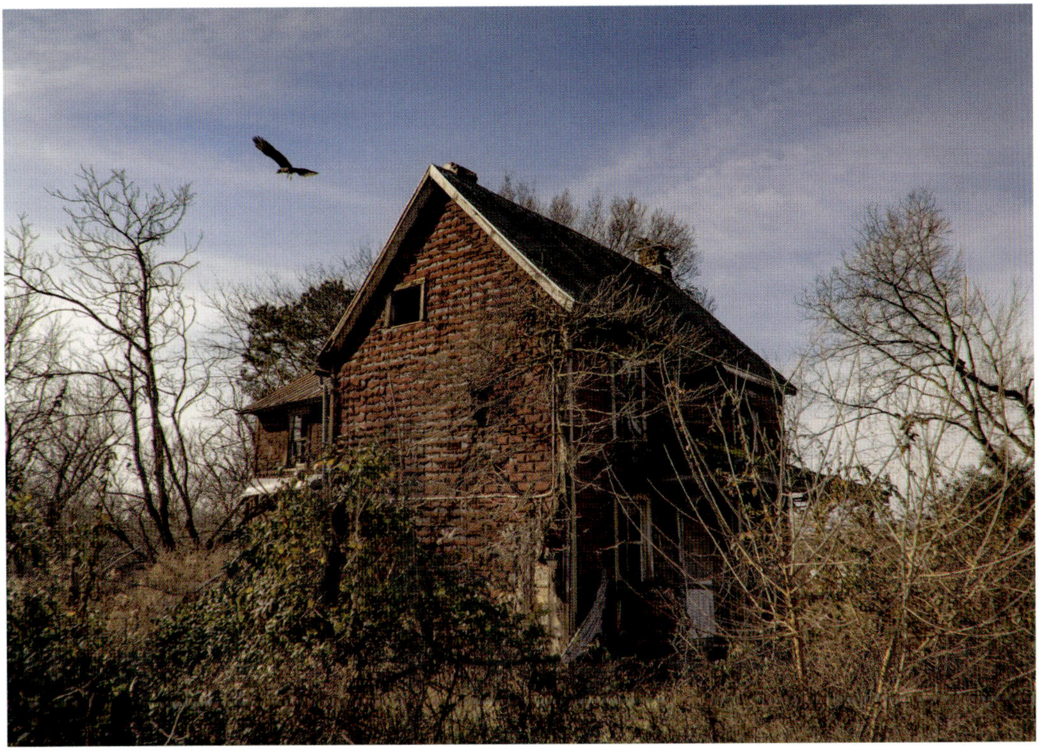

A creepy abandoned farm filled with animal cages in the plateau region. [*Rhea*]

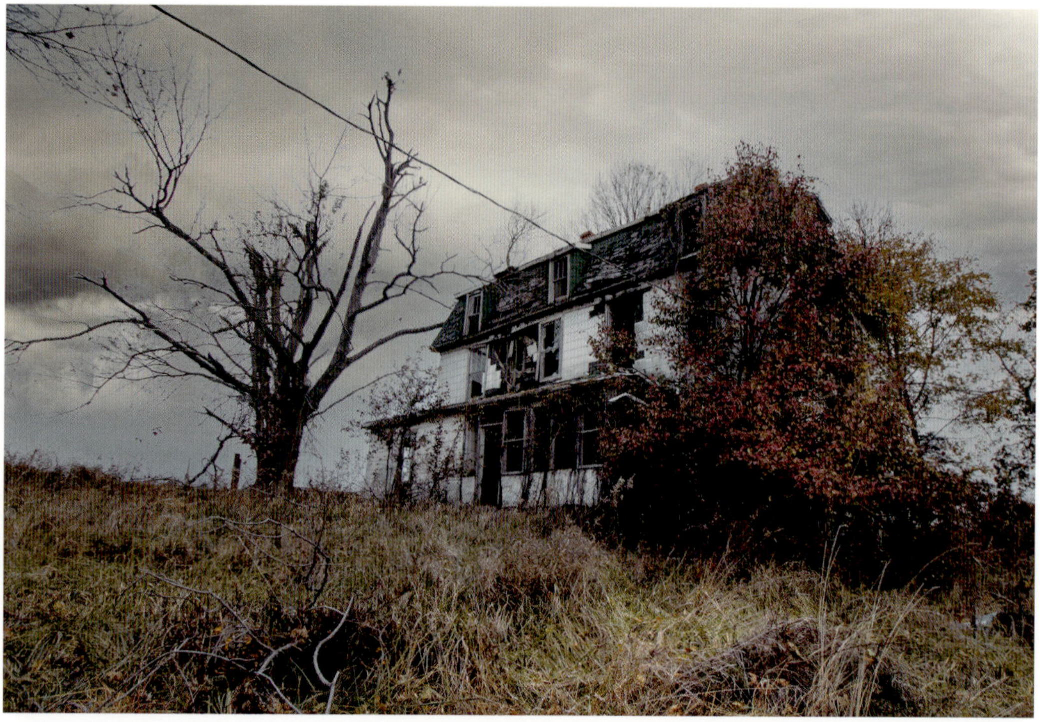

An abandoned Second Empire manor that was part of a dairy farm in the plateau region. [*Robyn*]

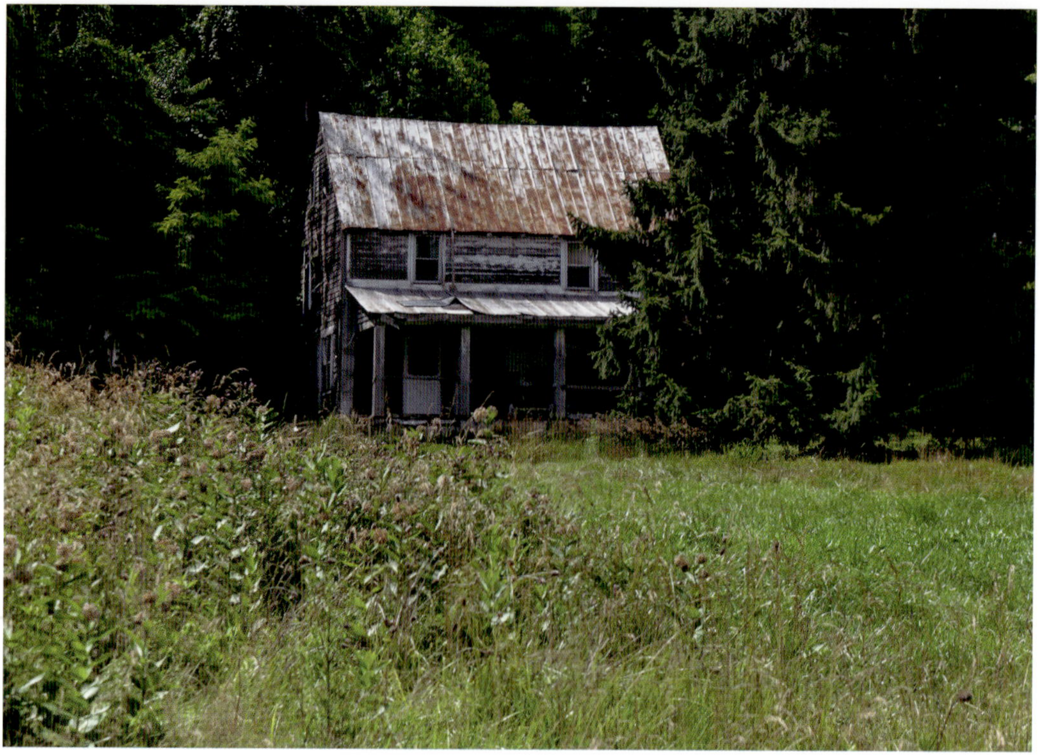

A vernacular farmhouse deteriorates in the western area of Maryland. [*Rhea*]

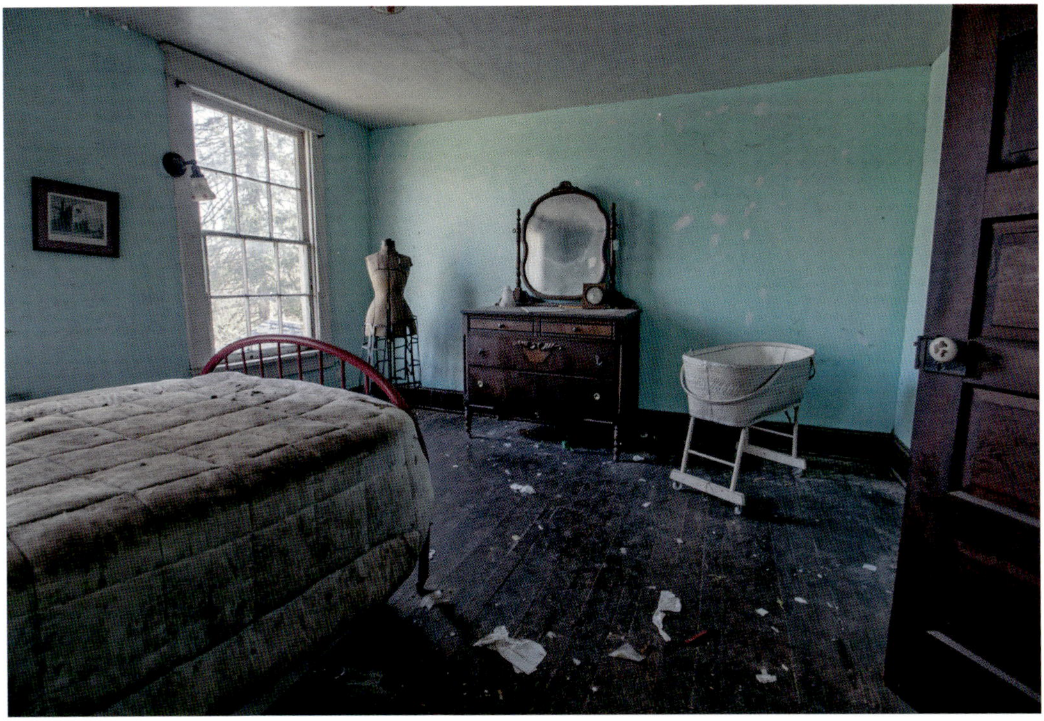

A Victorian dress form, a 1950s-era wicker bassinet, and an antique dresser decay amid lead-green painted walls. [*Rhea*]

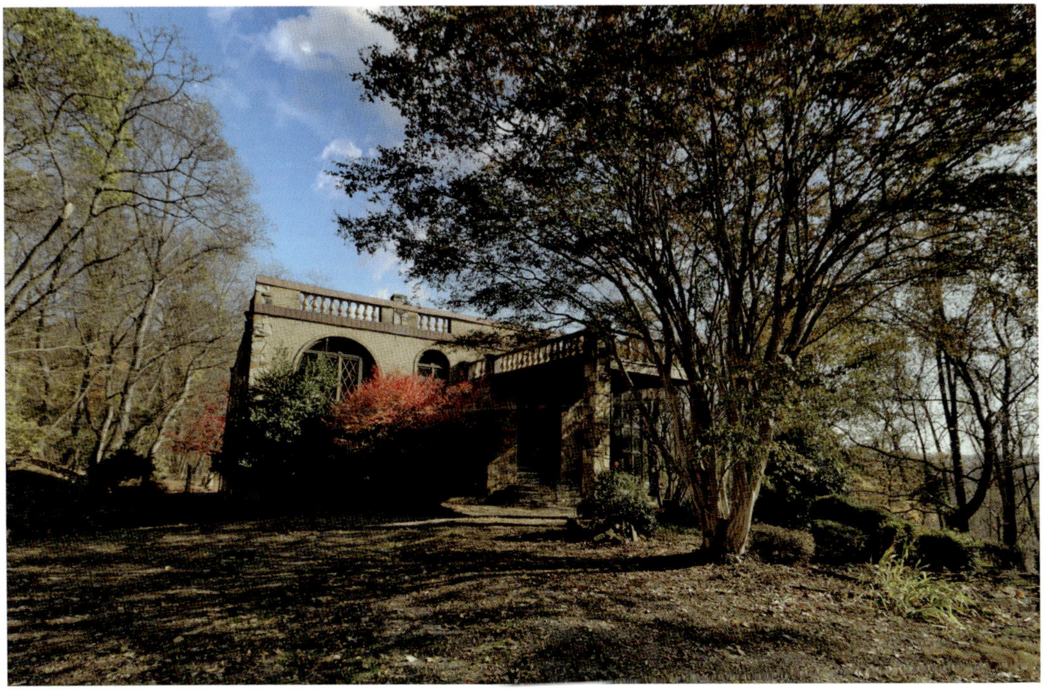

Nicknamed by many as a Playboy mansion, this house became abandoned after a landslide resulted in condemnation. [*Robyn*]

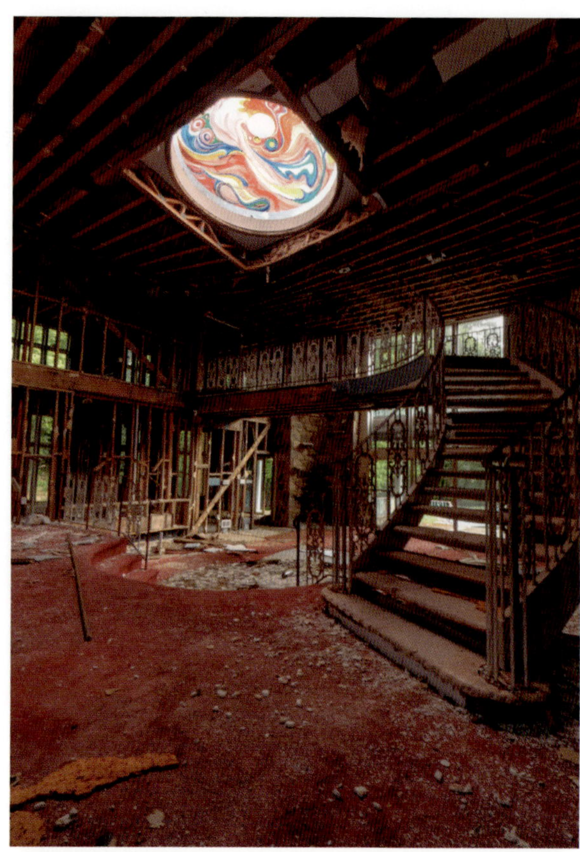

Left: The maroon staircase inside the Playboy mansion led to a psychedelic skylight. [*Robyn*]

Below: The back of the Playboy mansion. [*Rhea*]

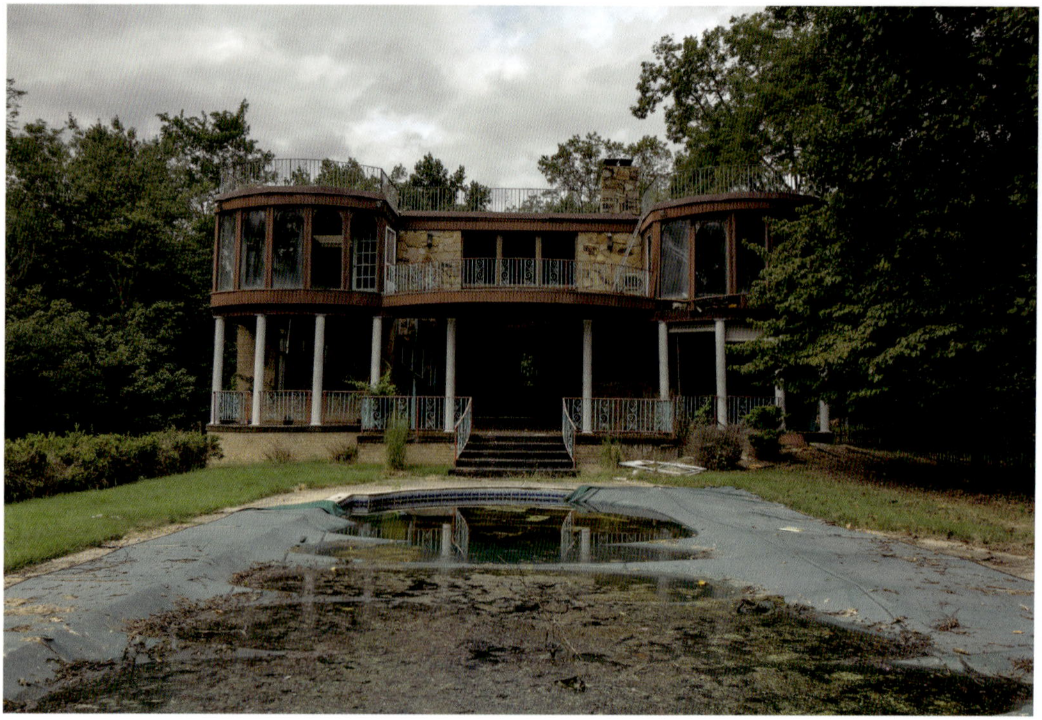

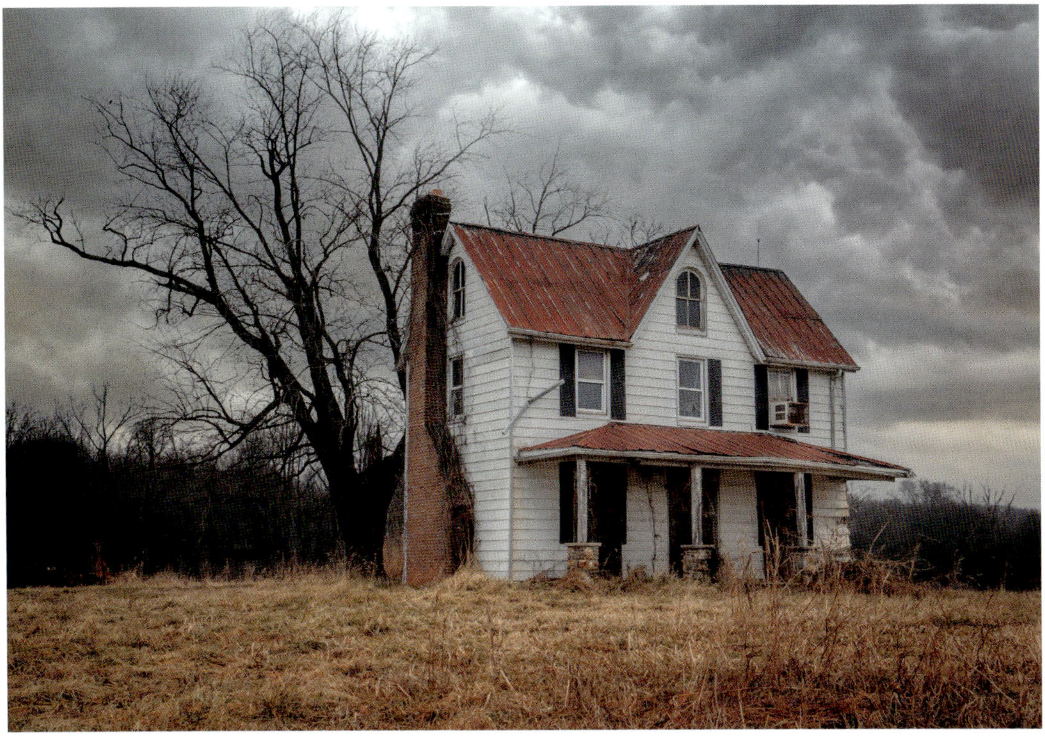

A Folk Victorian farmhouse in a field surrounded by housing developments. [*Rhea*]

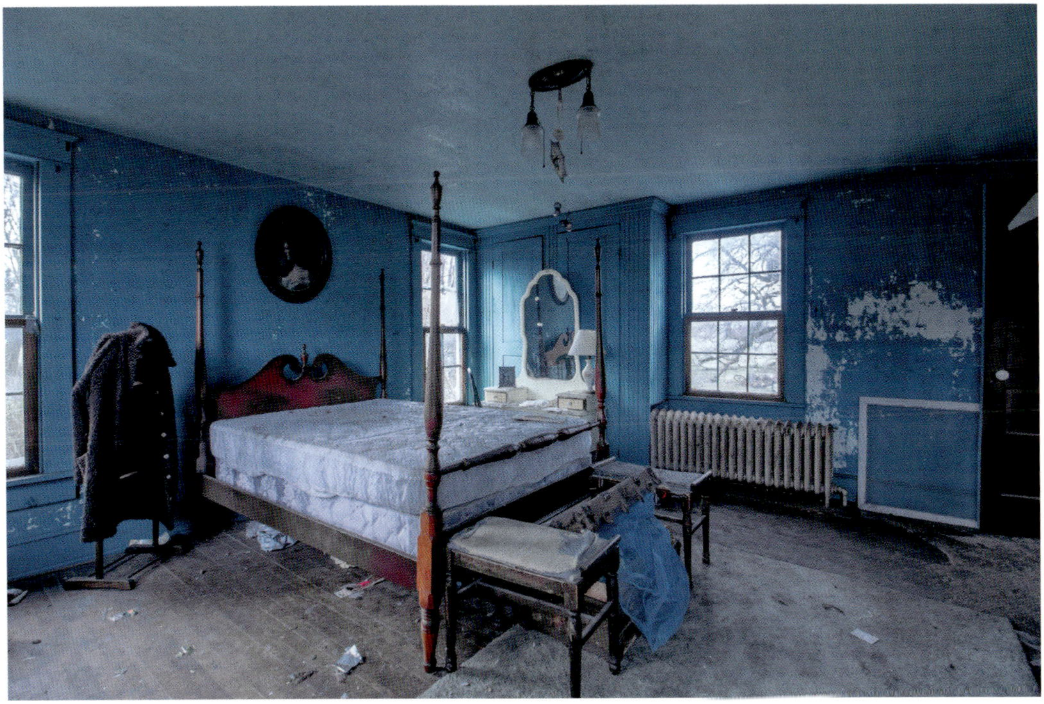

A woman's portrait, clothes, and letters remained among the antique furniture inside this nineteenth-century house. We are keeping historic information secret to protect the house. [*Robyn*]

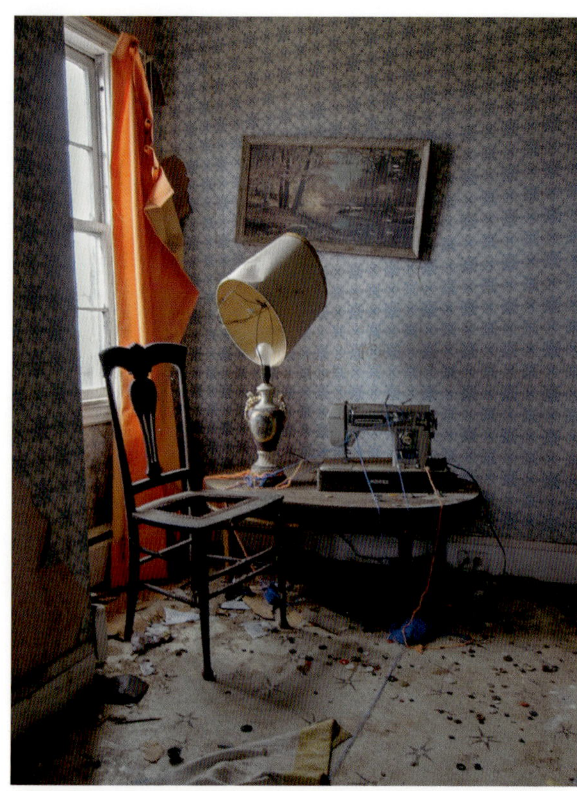

A sewing machine and a mid-20th century lamp remain in an abandoned folk Victorian farmhouse dubbed the "teacher's house" by explorers. The family must have been Catholic, because the house contained statues of Mary and Jesus. [*Robyn*]

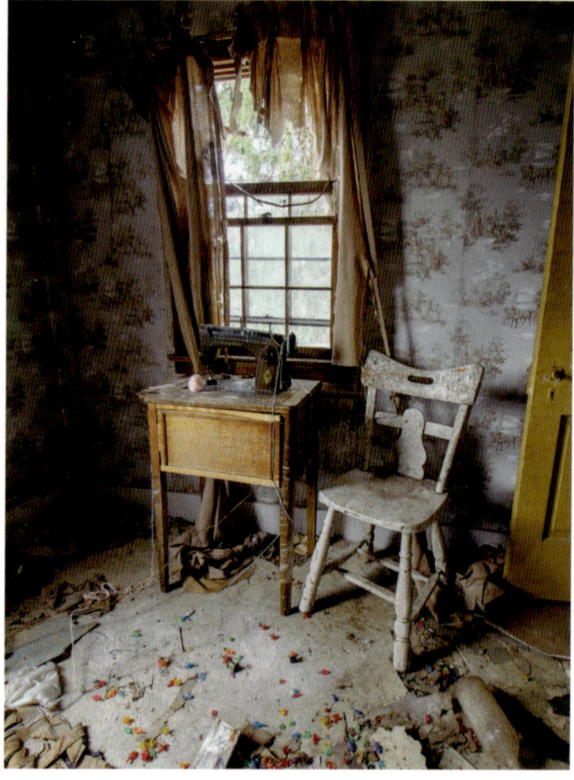

We found another sewing machine in the "teacher's house." [*Robyn*]

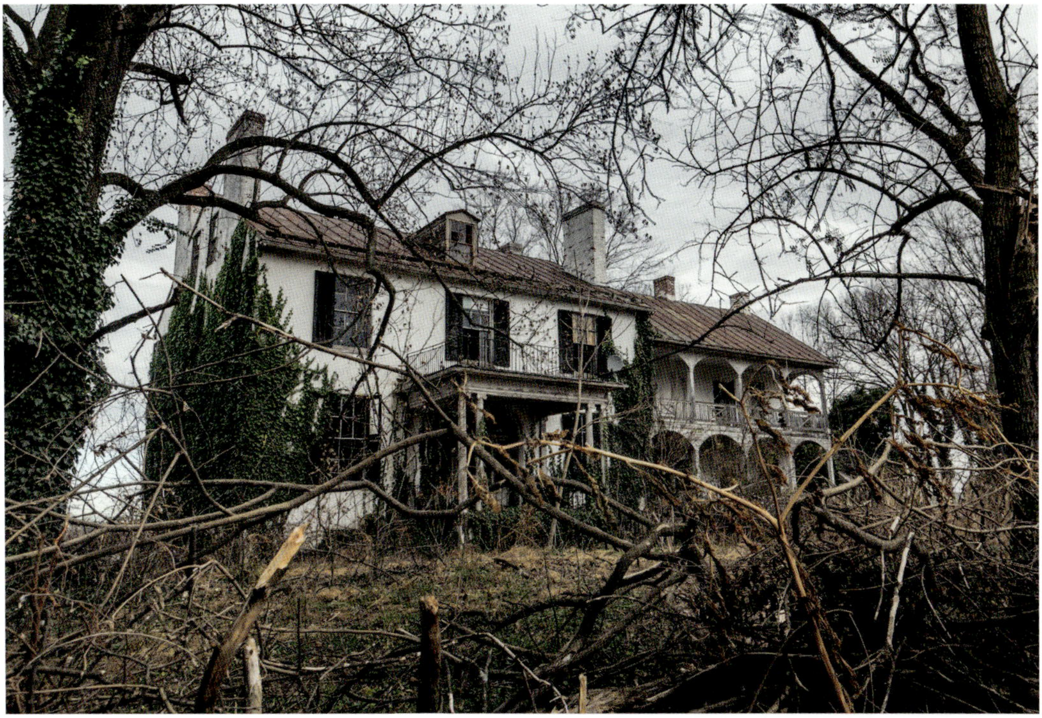

Above: Once home to the area's prominent residents, this federal style manor was built in 1815. The estate consists of at least twelve other structures in addition to the main house: a tenant house, a corn crib, a dairy barn, and other agricultural outbuildings. [*Rhea*]

Right: An antique Victorian pump organ slowly deteriorates inside an abandoned brick farm. [*Robyn*]

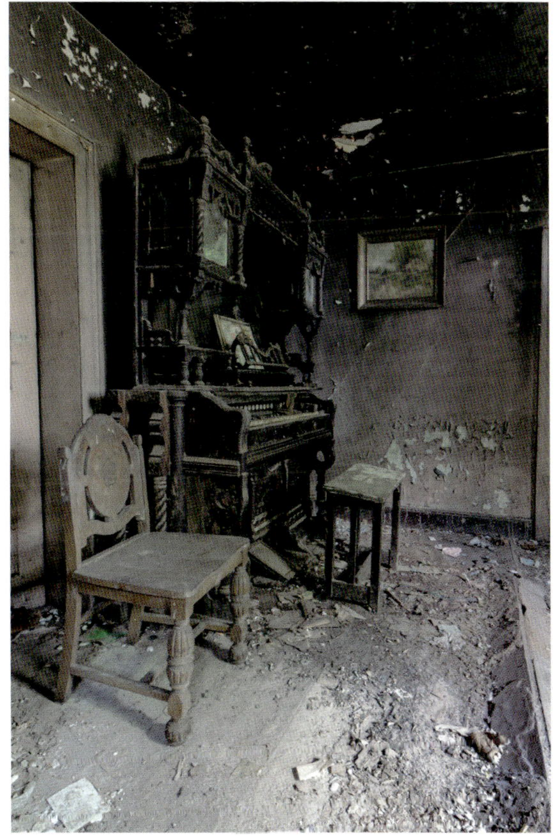

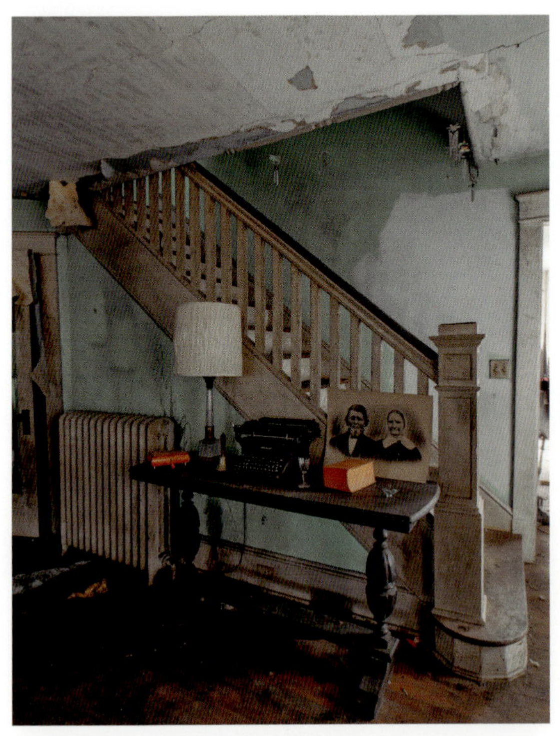

An antique Underwood typewriter with a nineteenth-century black-and-white photo in a 220-year-old manor. [*Robyn*]

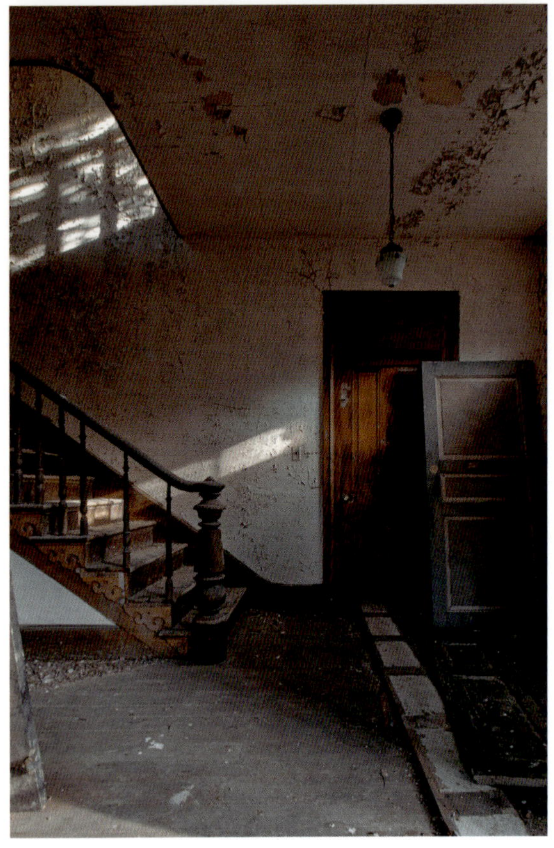

Light pours through the transom of an abandoned brick federal-style farm. [*Robyn*]

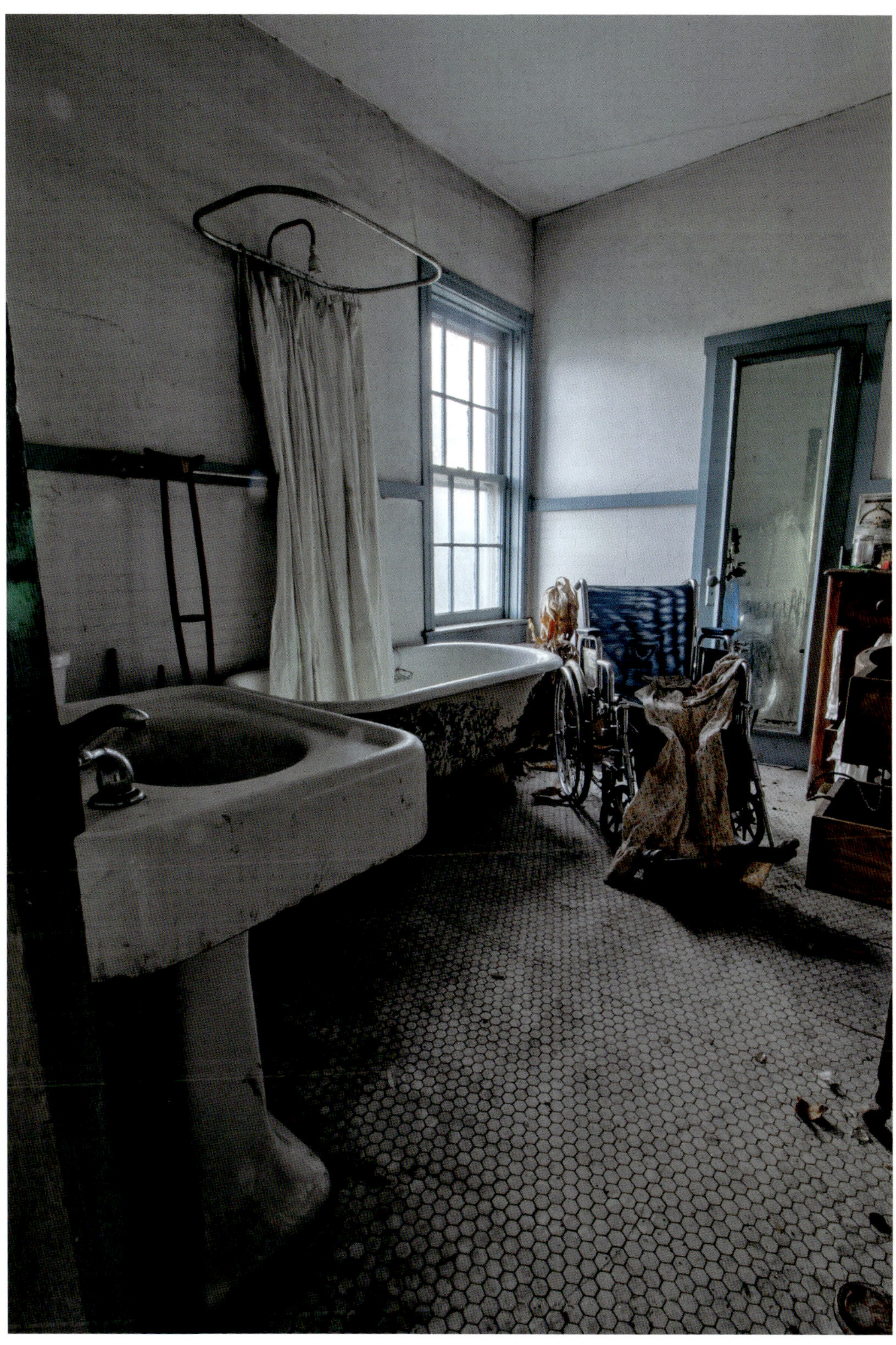

Notice the shape of a person on the mirror. It is likely condensation, but it feels ominous. [*Robyn*]

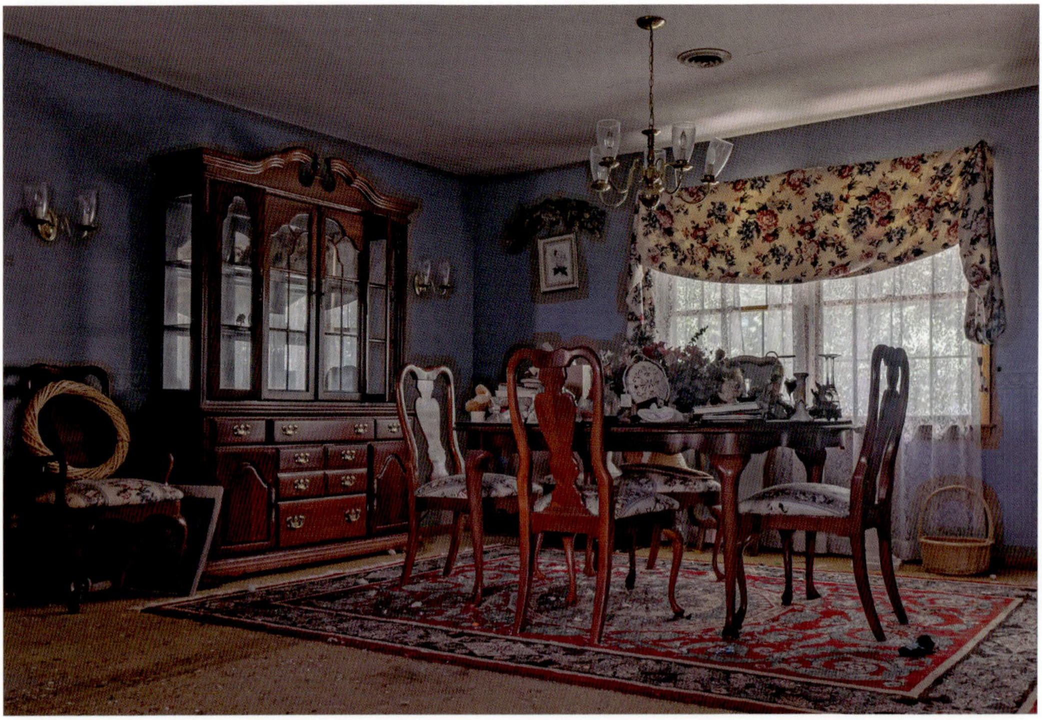

It's not often we explore houses that resemble eras that we've lived such as this mold-infested 1980s to 1990s style rancher bursting with trash. [*Rhea*]

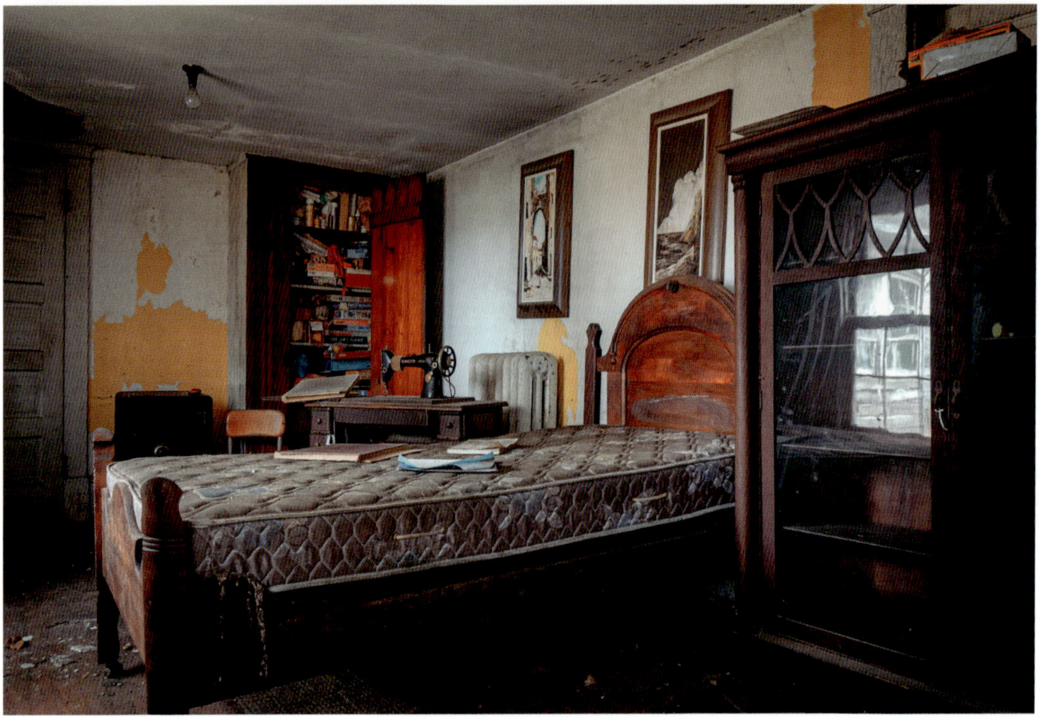

An antique sewing machine and bed in an abandoned house. [*Rhea*]

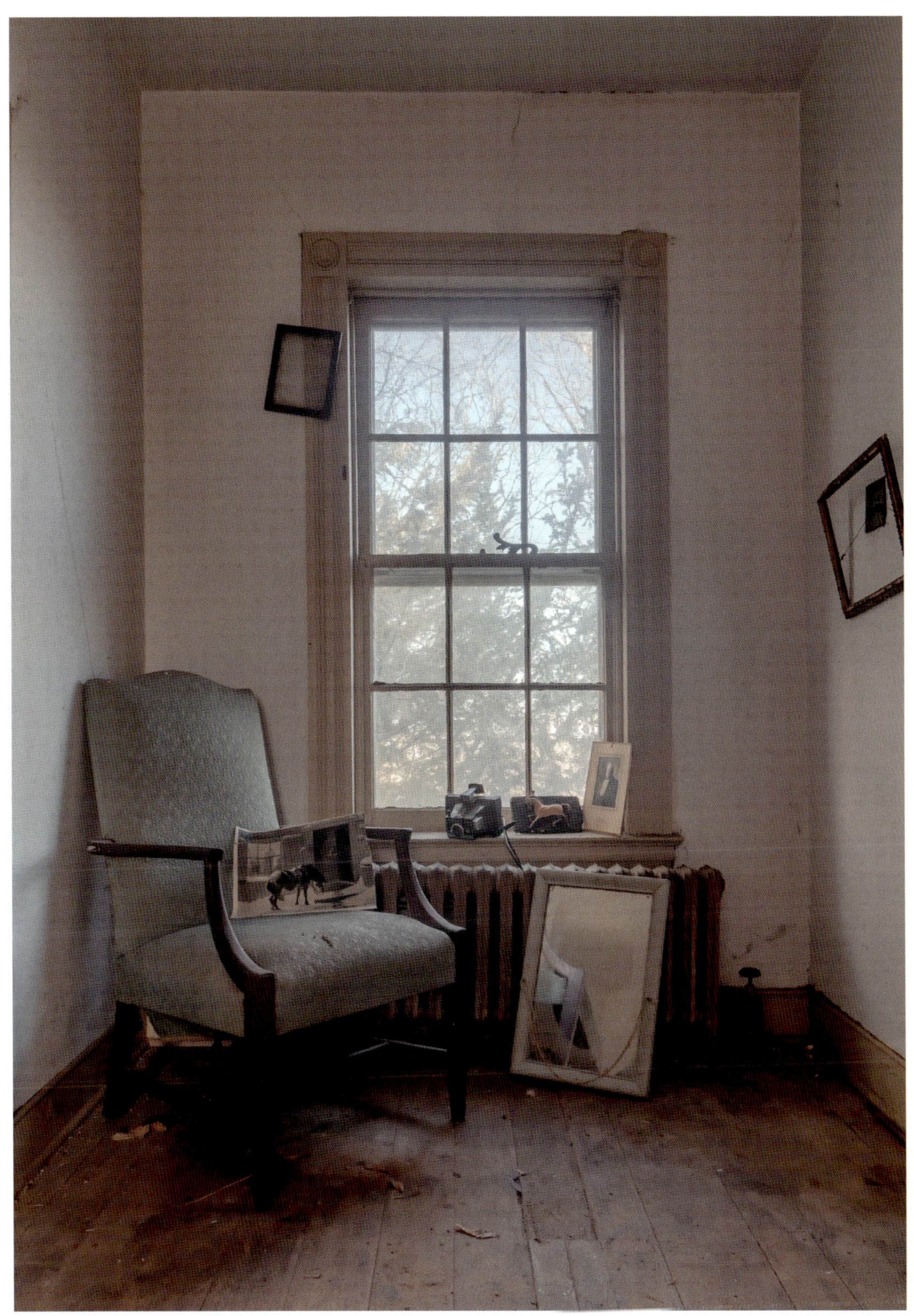

These antiques linger long after their owners have departed this time capsule home. [*Rhea*]

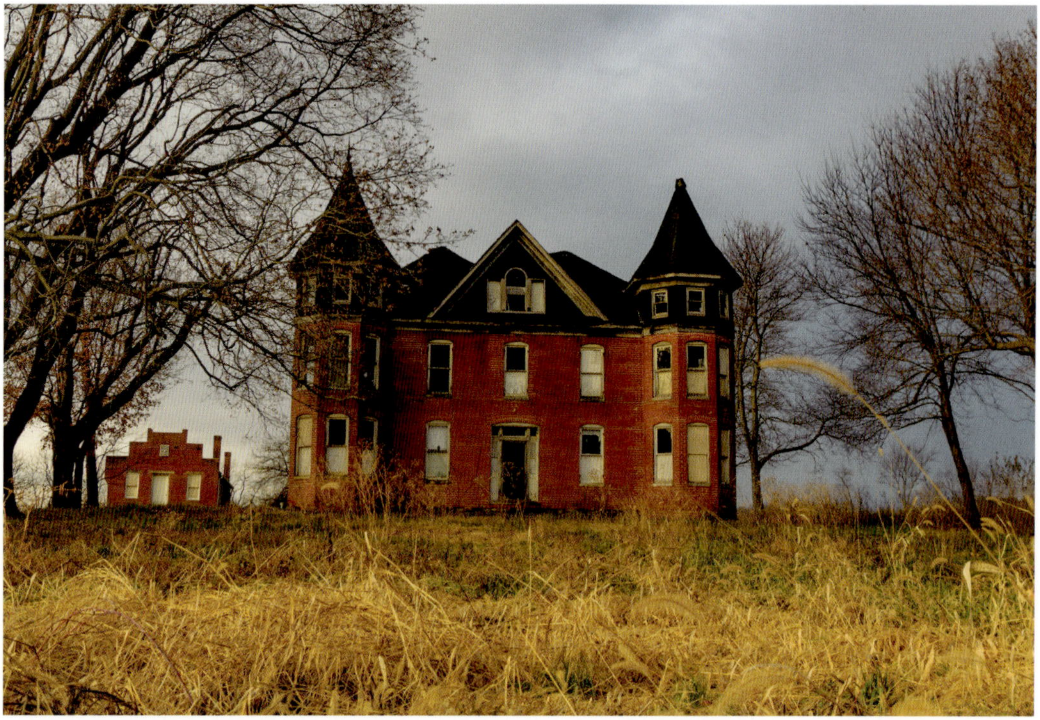

Built in 1880, this Gothic two-and-a-half-story-brick Victorian mansion bears octagonal corner turrets that loom ominously over the sky. [*Rhea*]

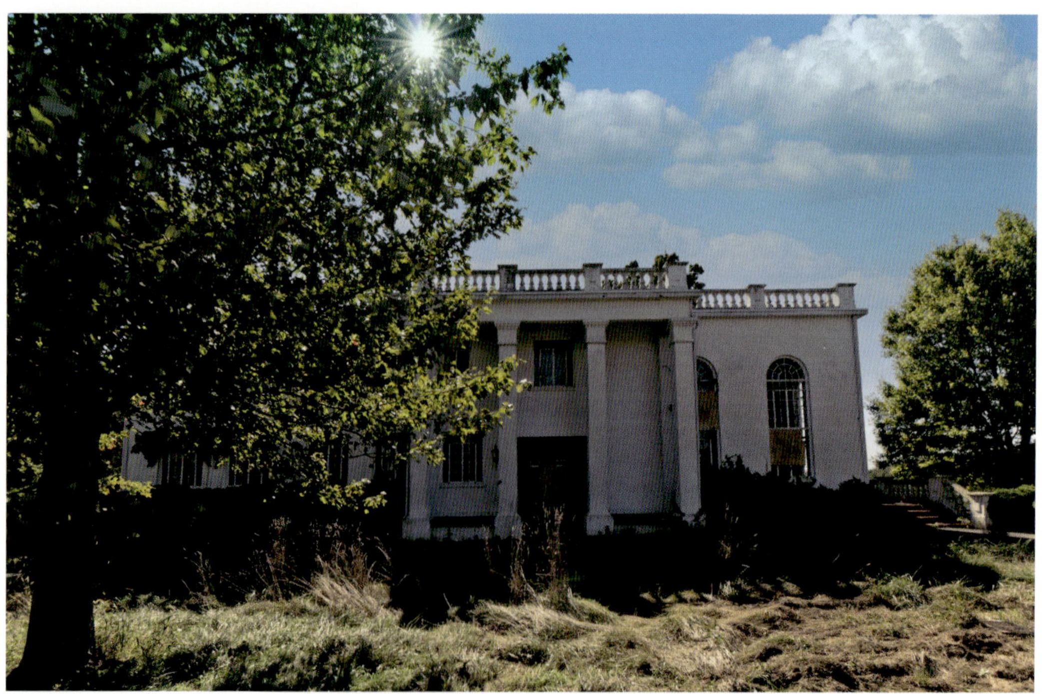

This Greek revival mansion is no longer abandoned. When it was, kids and looters vandalized it. Out of respect, we will not disclose any historical information since it has been renovated and reoccupied. [*Robyn*].

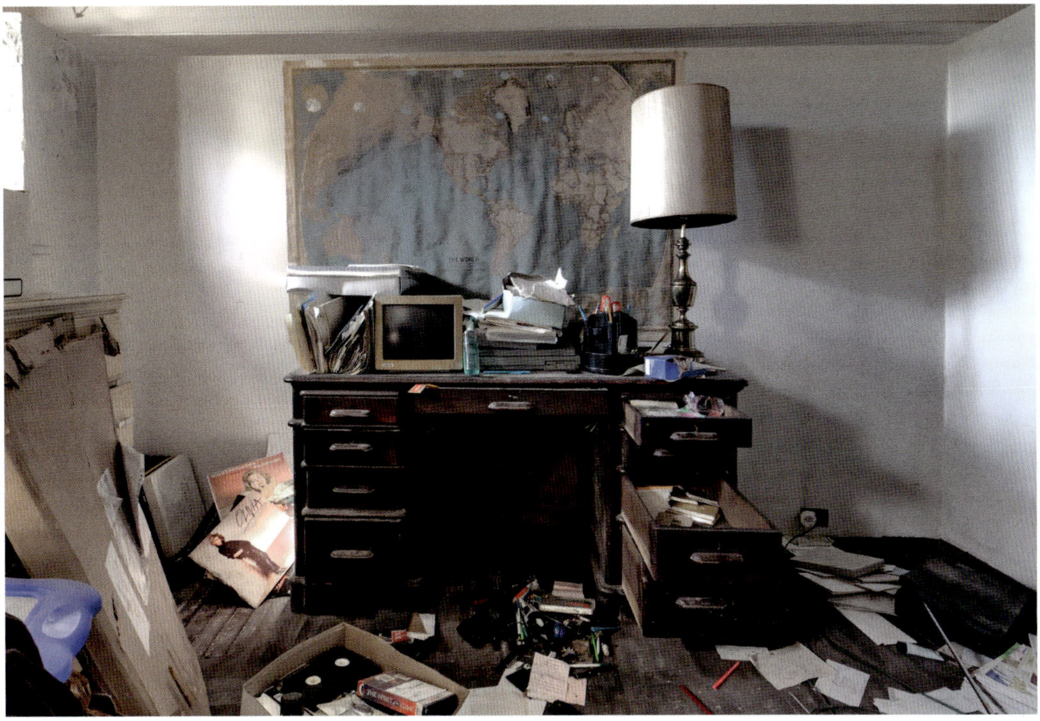

Looters trashed the basement office inside an abandoned Greek revival mansion. (Note: This property is no longer abandoned.) [*Robyn*]

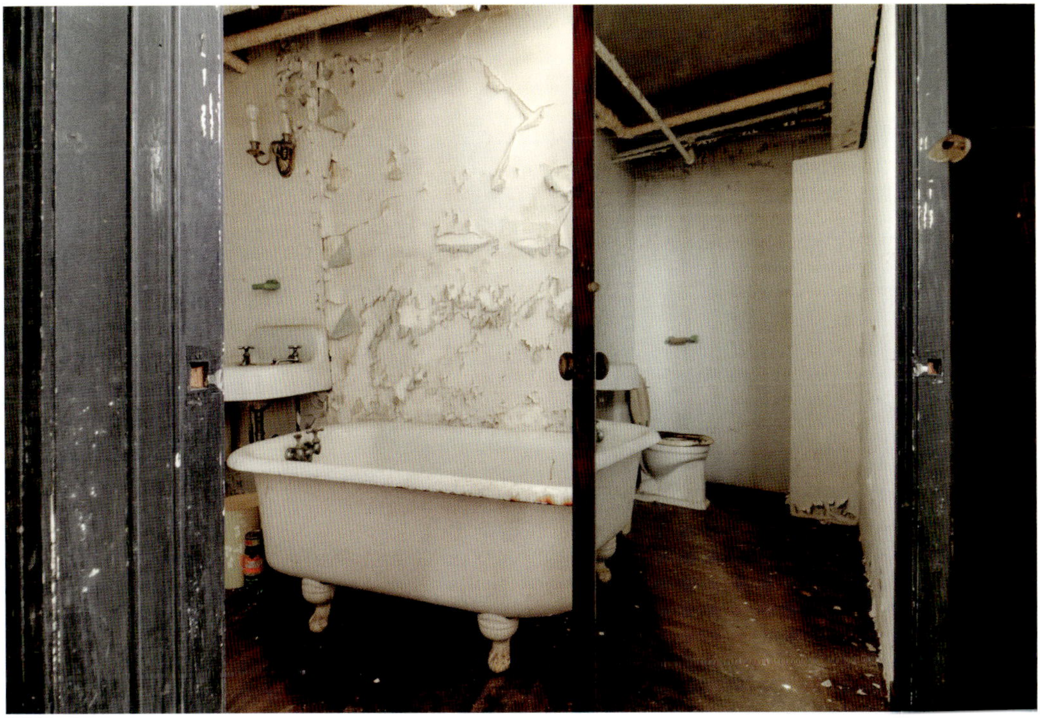

We discovered a dead mouse in this bear-claw bathtub. [*Robyn*]

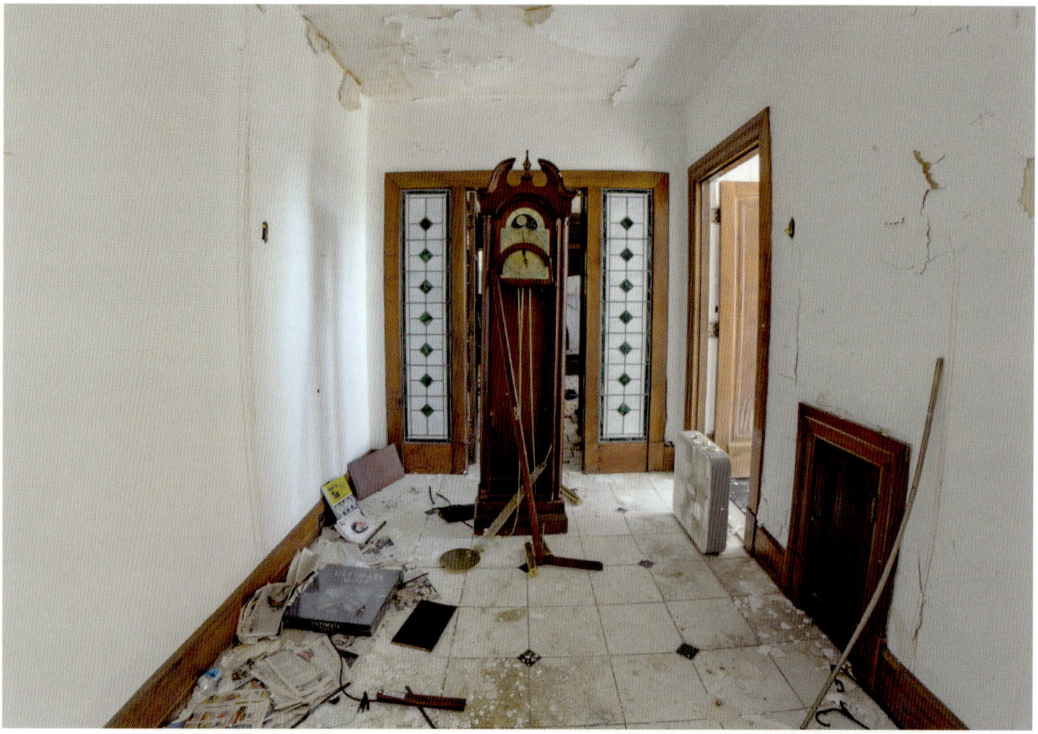

A grandfather clock dragged into a foyer by looters of the formerly abandoned mansion. [*Rhea*]

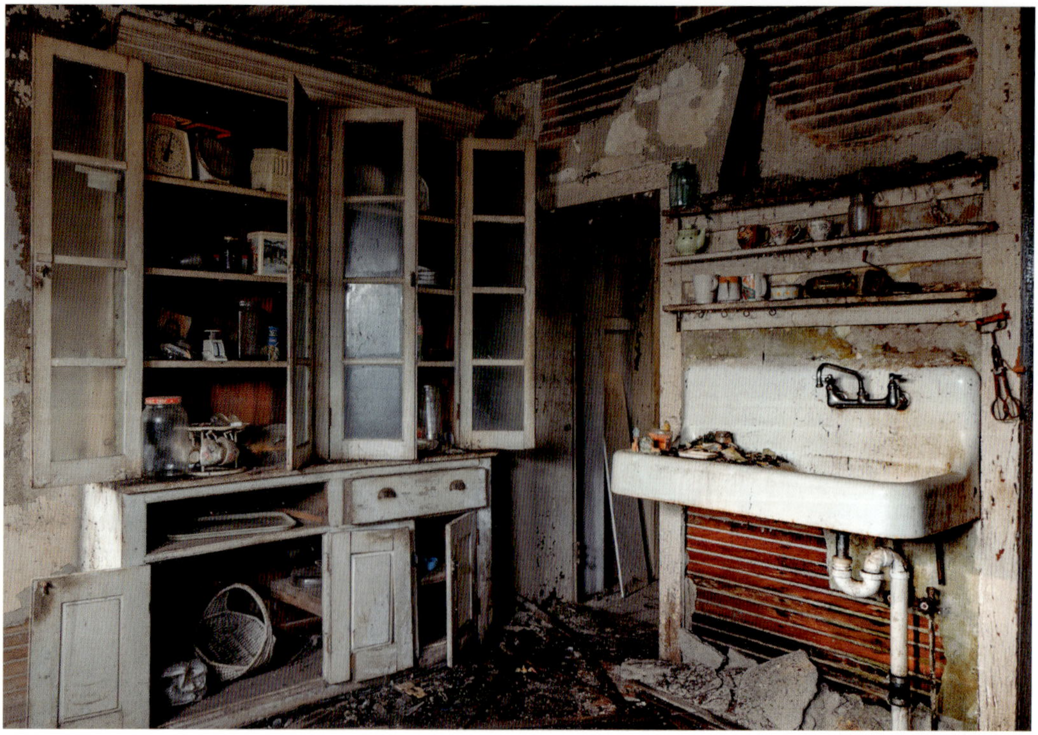

Things remaining in the kitchen of a nineteenth-century house. [*Rhea*]

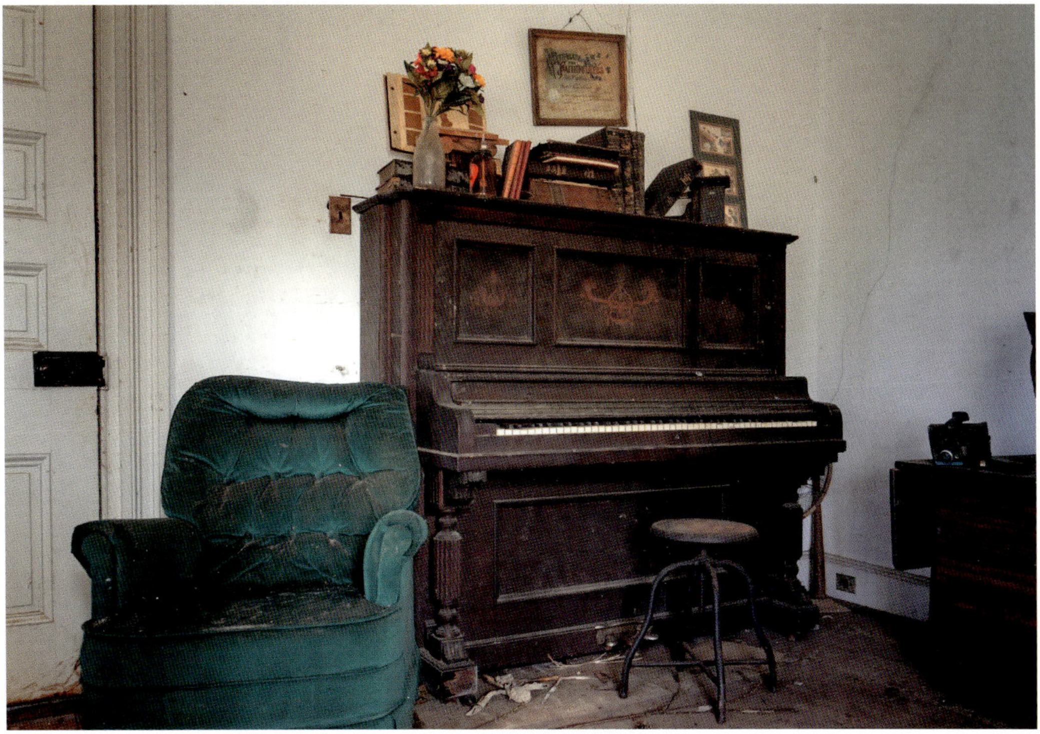

There is a saying that every abandoned house has a piano and at least a chair. [*Rhea*]

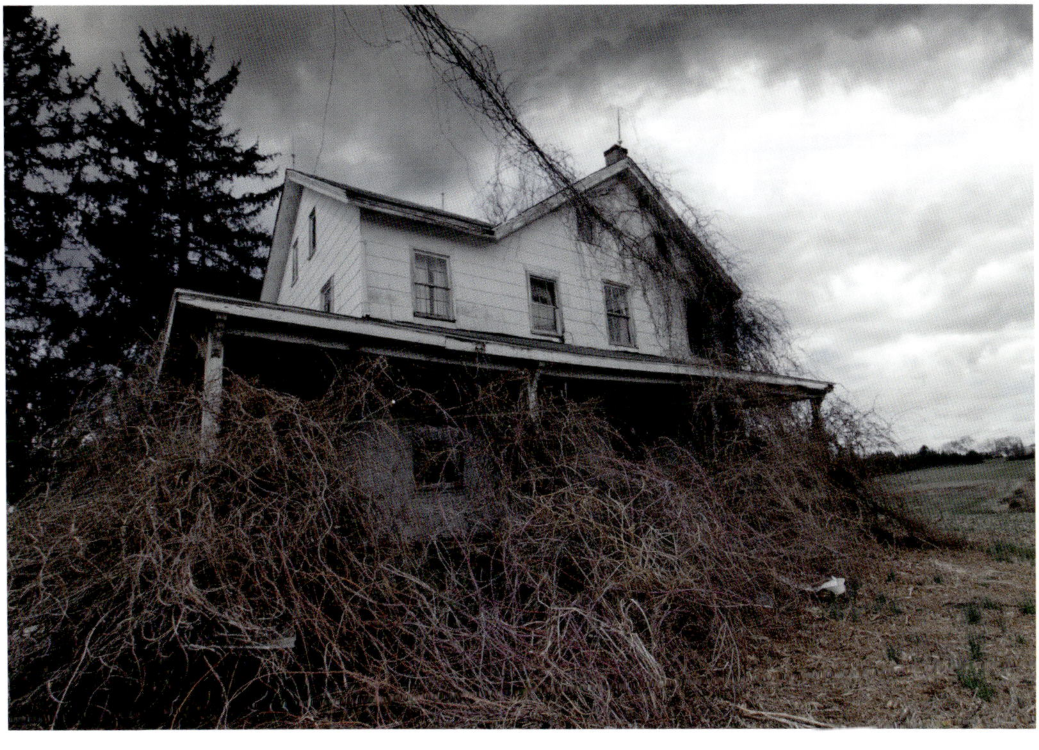

This large vernacular late Victorian-era farmhouse is blanketed by creepers. [*Robyn*]

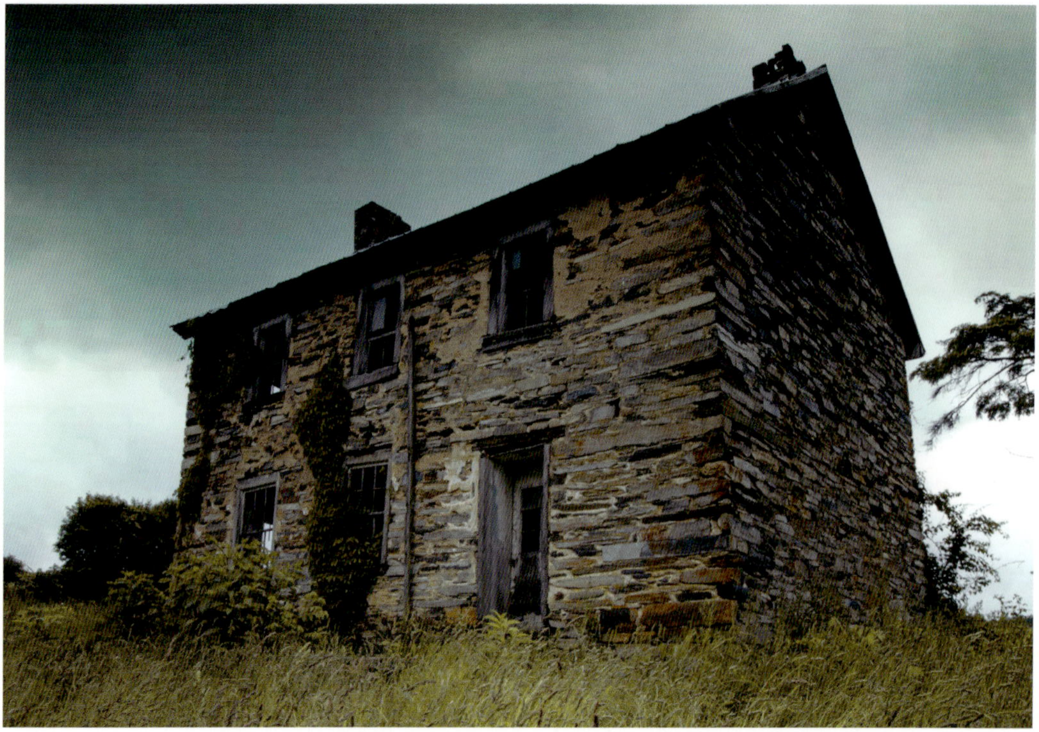

An abandoned stone house in the western region of the state is now home to a family of birds. [*Robyn*]

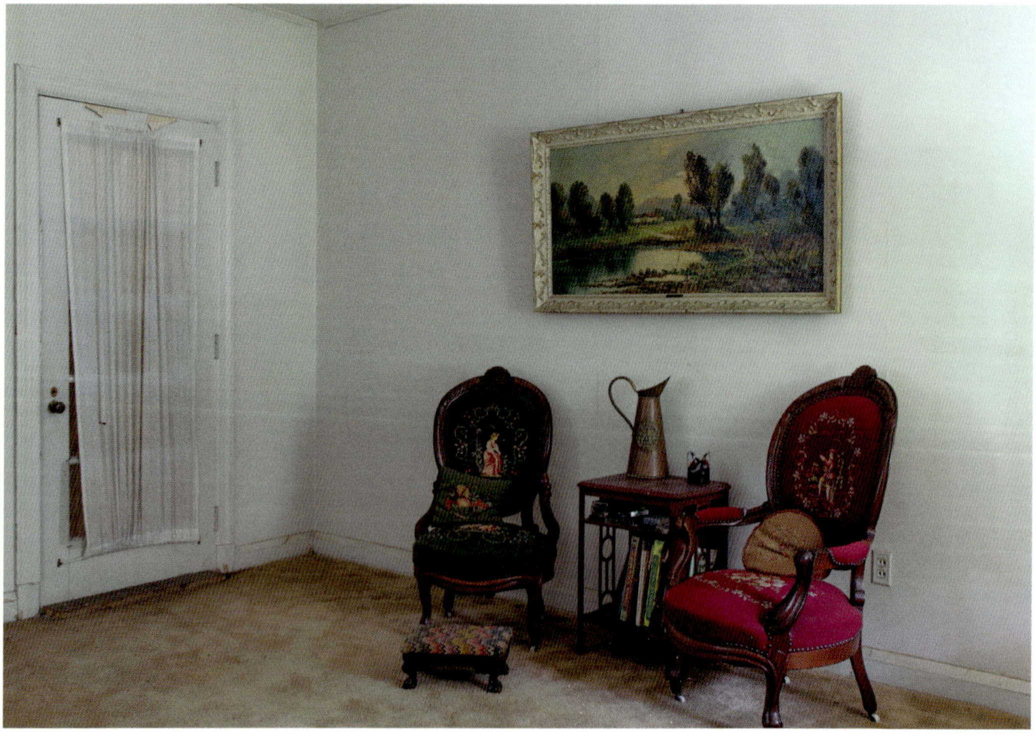

Vintage chairs and art left in a historic cottage. [*Rhea*]

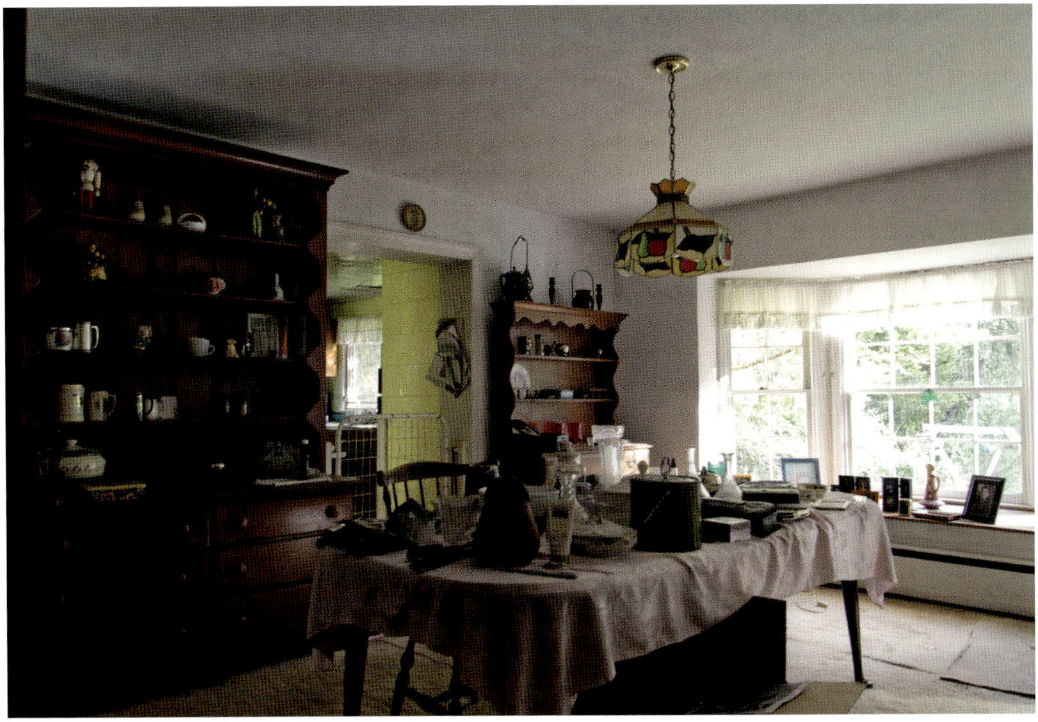

Someone left glassware arranged on an antique dining room table. [*Robyn*]

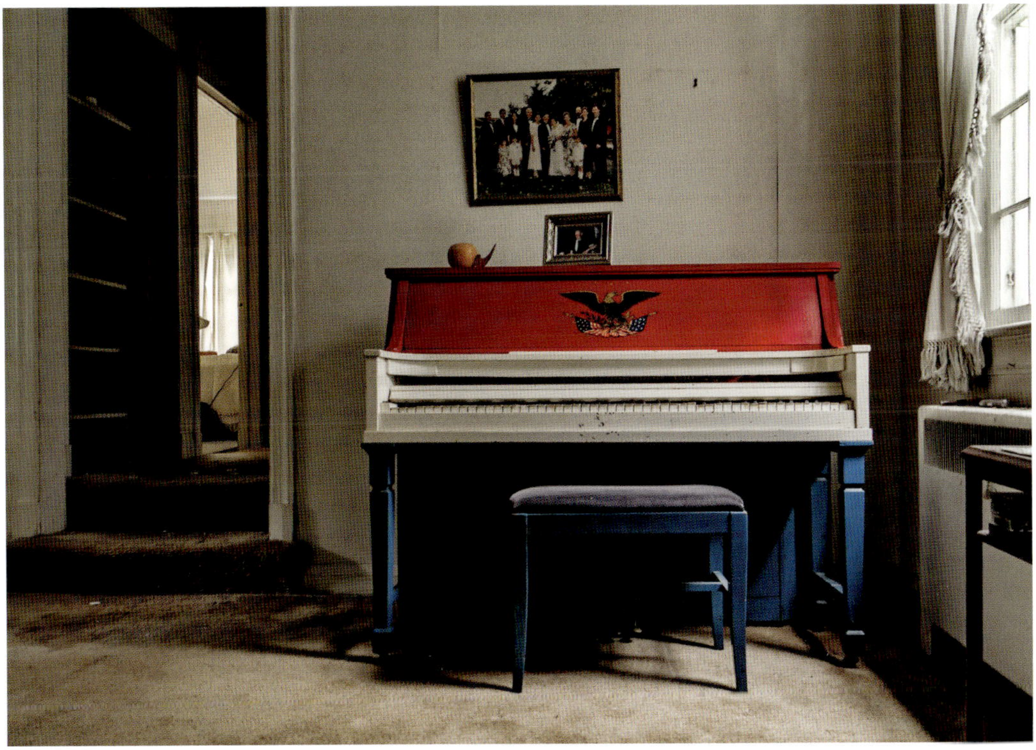

A patriotic piano left inside a large, historic, late 1930s bungalow. [*Robyn*]

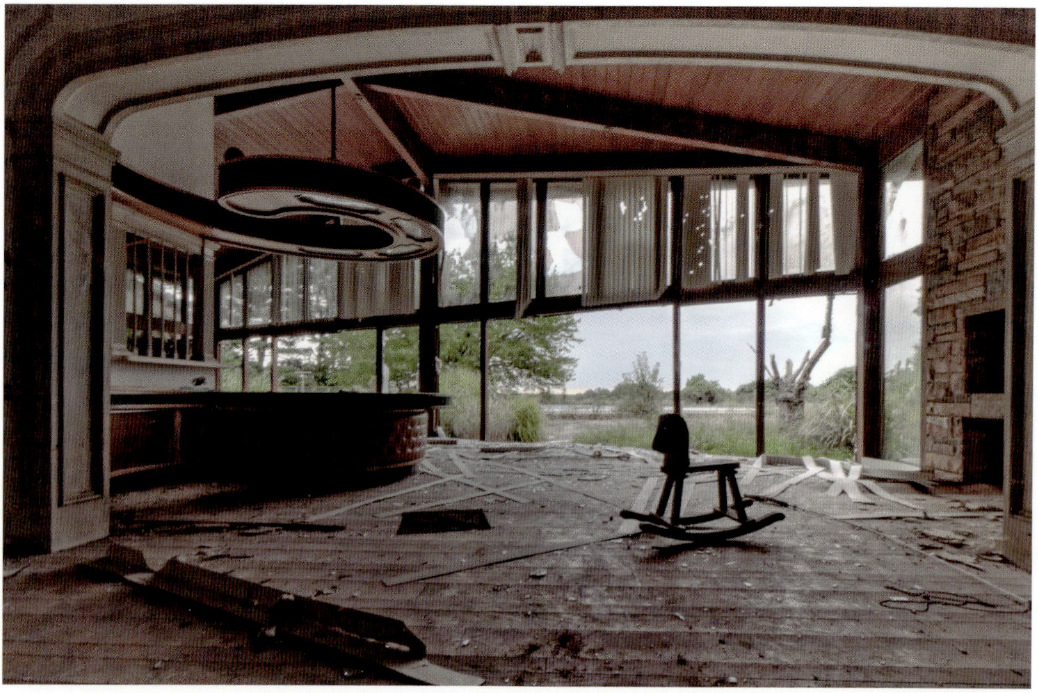

Vandals busted the patio door glass of this mansion that supposedly became abandoned due to being seized by the government because of criminal activity. [*Robyn*]

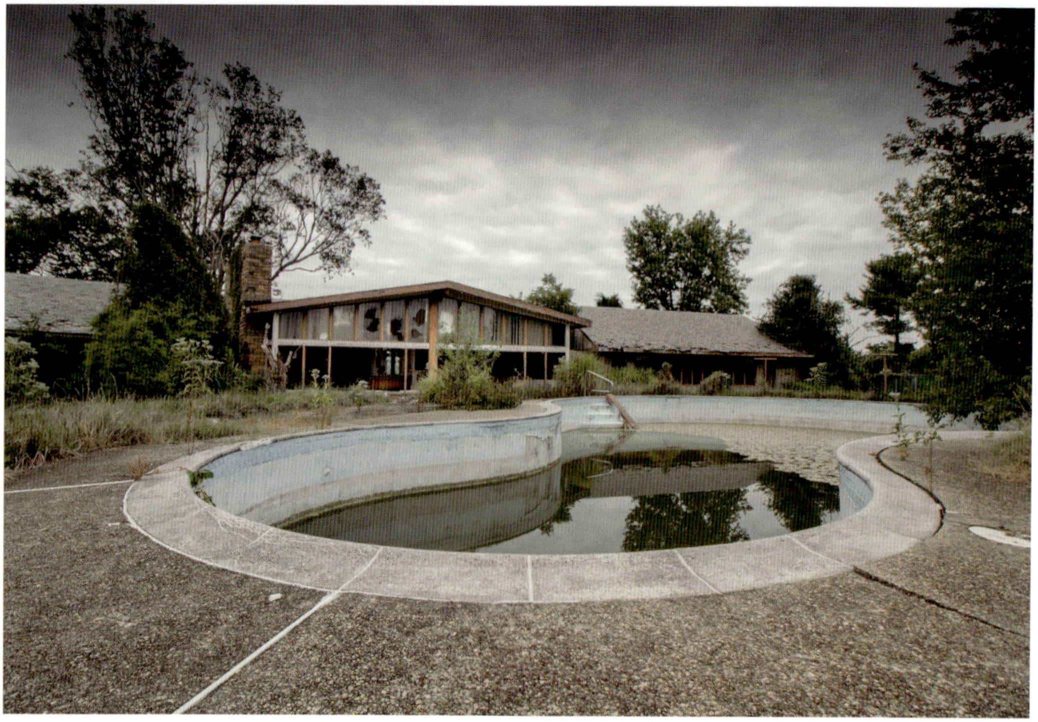

The back of an abandoned mansion that according to rumors the government seized because of criminal activity. [*Robyn*]

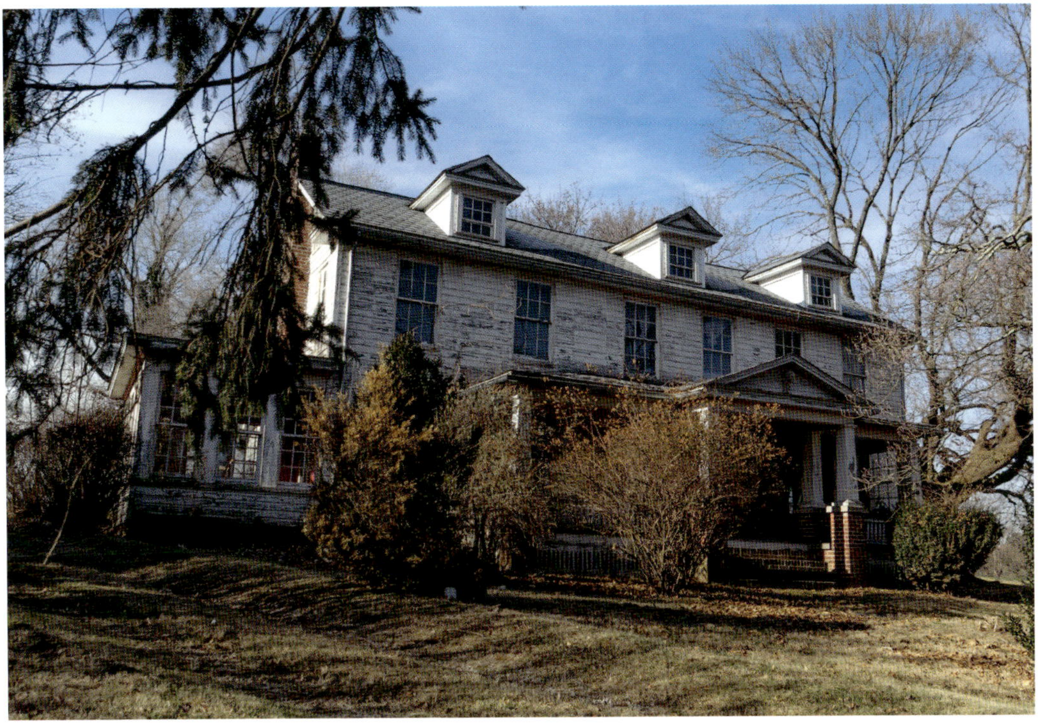

This grand manor is more than 200 years old and is being renovated. [*Rhea*]

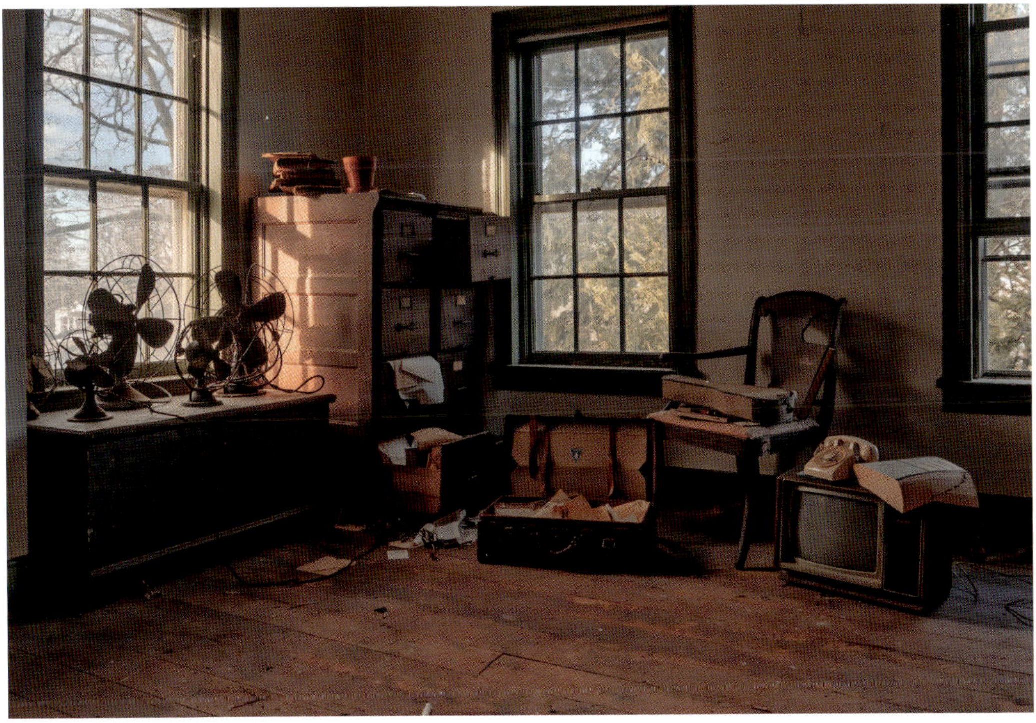

The morning light illuminates these vintage fans through the lead-glass windows of this historic abandoned home. [*Rhea*]

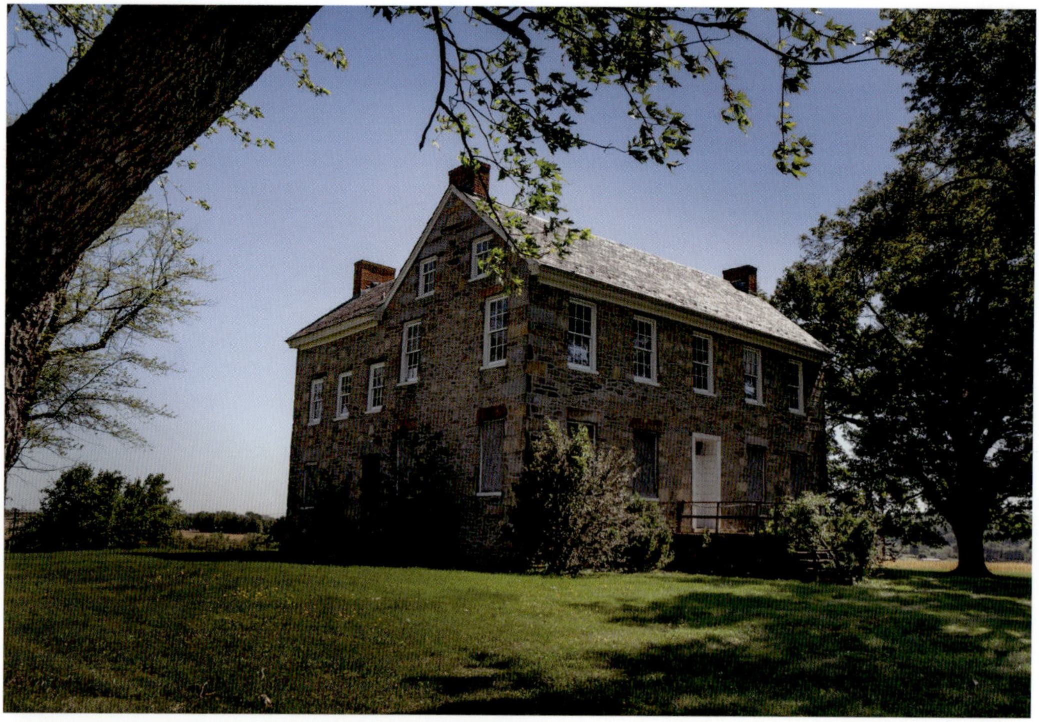

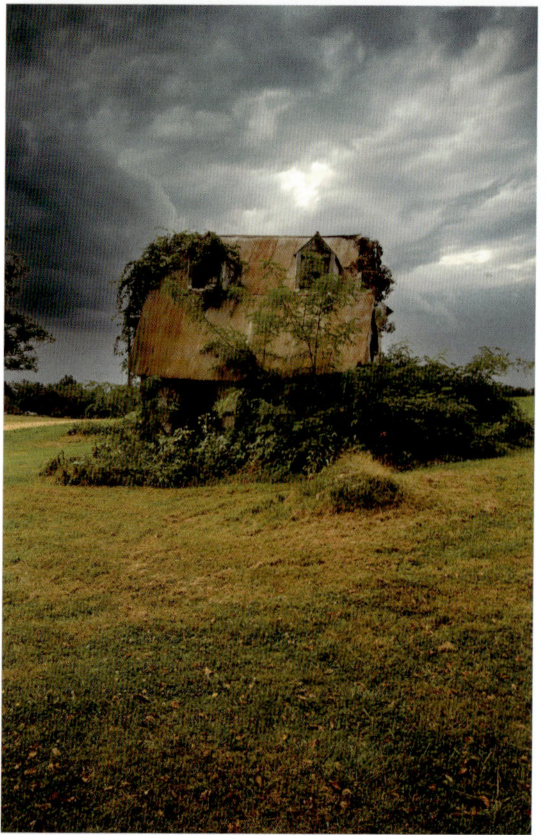

Above: We were not able to discover the history of this historic stone house, but we believe it likely dates to the eighteenth century. [*Rhea*]

Left: Nature has blanketed this tiny house in western Maryland. [*Robyn*]

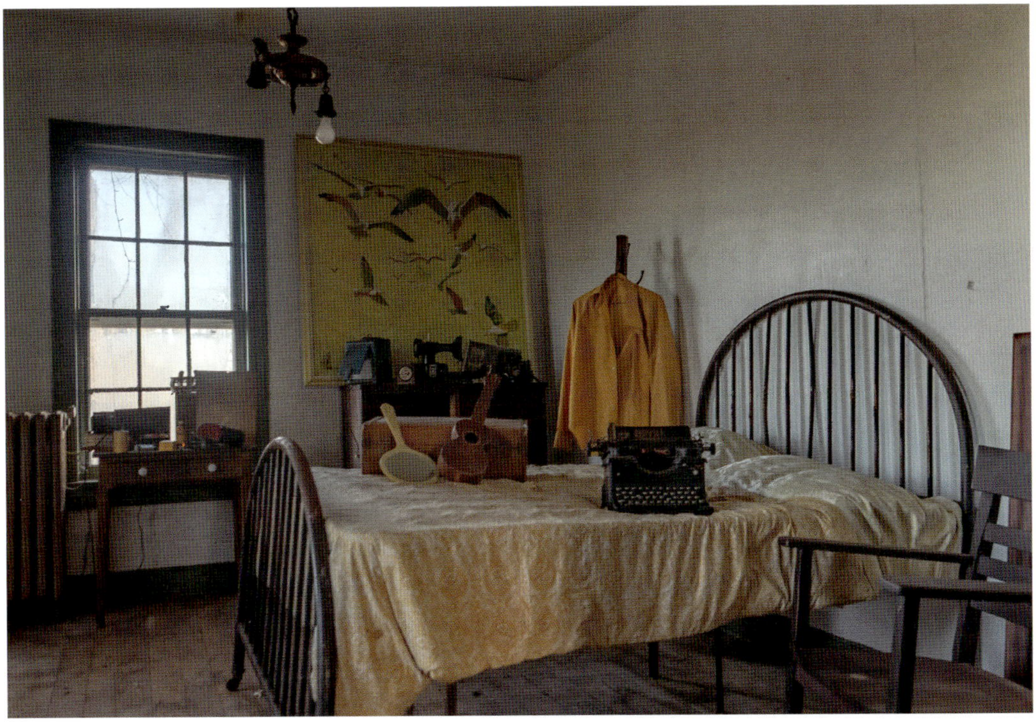

Above: This abandoned historic house brims with antiques, relics, and raccoon feces. [*Rhea*]

Right: Built in the late 1800s, this Victorian farm is hidden from view by overgrown trees. We could not discover any historic information on it. [*Robyn*]

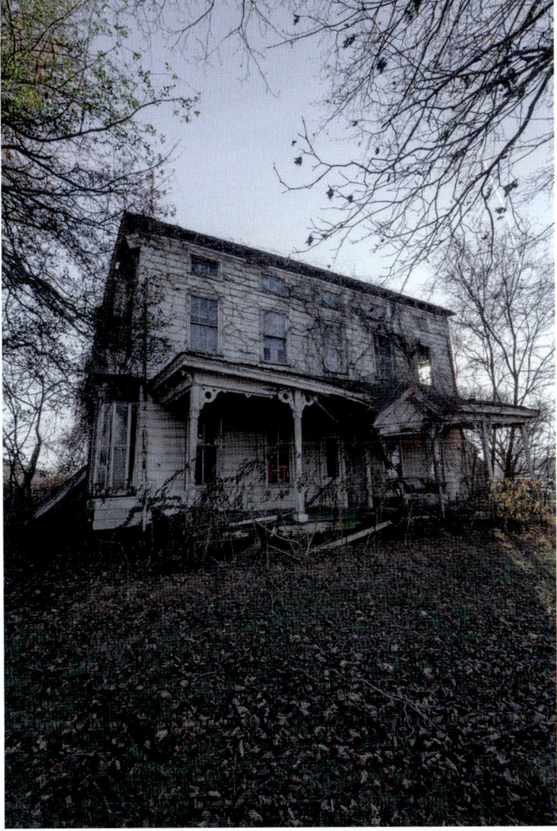

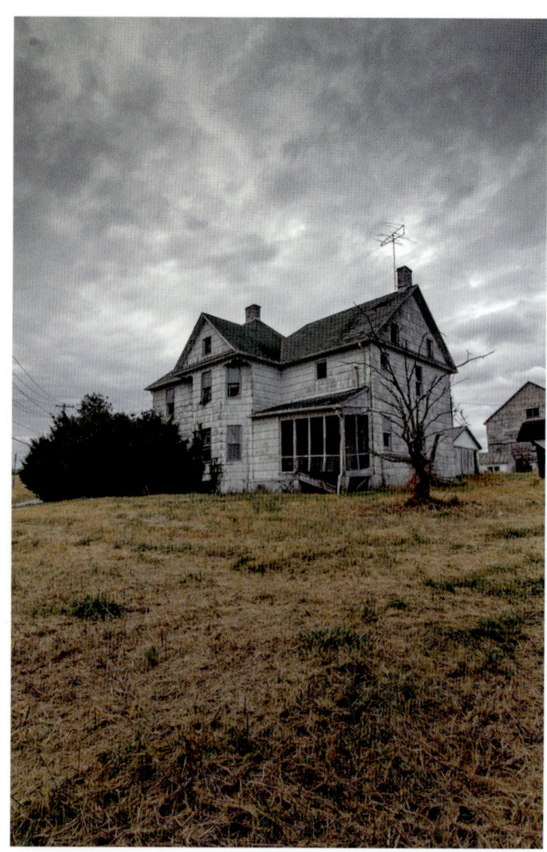

Left: Sadly, warring political graffiti covers the walls of this large Queen Anne style farmhouse. [*Robyn*]

Below: We find many abandoned farmhouses like this Folk Victorian while driving the backroads. Hay fills the halls of this old home. [*Robyn*]

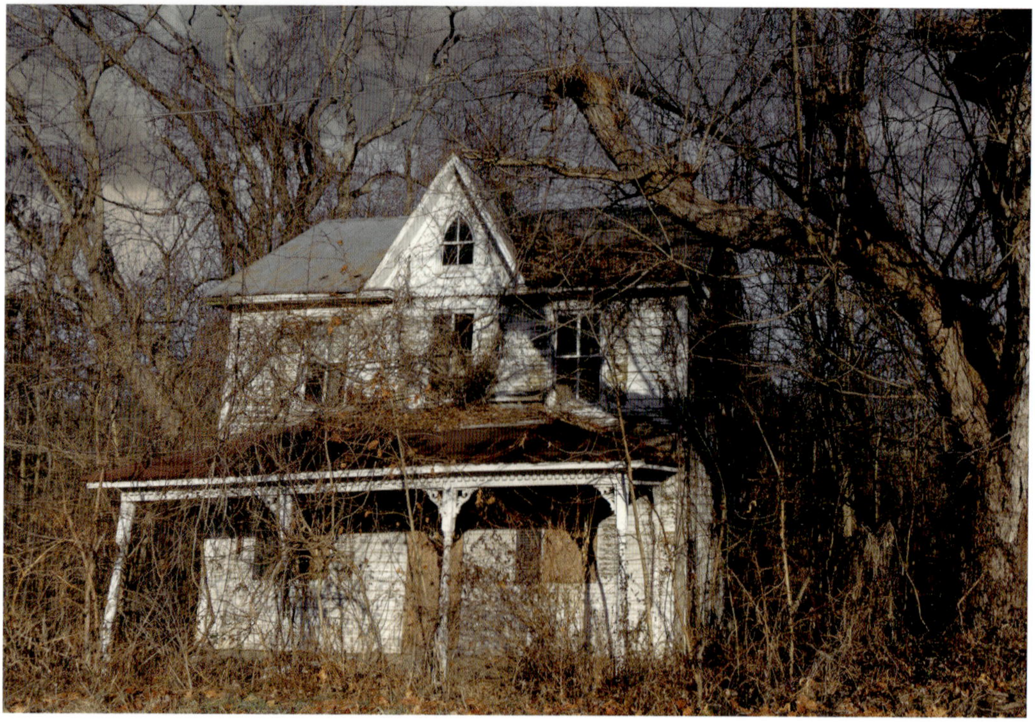

3

FARMS OF EASTERN SHORE, MARYLAND

Maryland stretches east into the Delmarva peninsula that is enveloped by the Chesapeake Bay and the Atlantic Ocean that it shares with Delaware and Virginia. Climate change has caused many farmers to abandon their homes on the Eastern Shore of Maryland. Scientists are studying how they can mitigate the crisis to save as much farmland as possible as the shore possesses many of the oldest farms in the country, dating back to the mid 1600s. Of course, the state and nation depend on the region's farming and seafood industry. The area also plays a key role in African American history. Climate change is causing the area to lose "thousands of acres of farmland" because of saltwater intrusion. Salt is infiltrating groundwater, and rising sea water is flooding the land, creating tidal marshes and killing forests, which are buffers against hurricanes. The salt infiltration renders the land futile for farming. Calculating these risks, many farmers moved west to the Piedmont area to farm.

In addition to climate change, it is vital to consider the region's place in history. Europeans first settled the Delmarva Peninsula in the 1500s, encountering three indigenous Algonquian tribes: "the Piscataway on the Western Shore, who left the area in 1697; and the Nanticoke and Pocomoke-Assateague on the Eastern Shore, who migrated westward in the 1740s." The Susquehannock lived there as well; but the Iroquois Nations captured them in 1675.

For colonists, agriculture served as the primary mode of economy. In the 1700s, Delmarva farms served as the "breadbasket of the American Revolution." Due to its key location to the water, goods could be smuggled past crown loyalists to Washington's troops. It is vital to understand that the crops were not harvested by paid workers. Slaves harvested the wheat and also tobacco, a back-breaking product.

Maryland's farmers also relied on indentured servants. This system provided them free labor and provided them with great wealth.

Amid the brutality of slavery on the Eastern Shore, two of the most influential figures in African American history were born: Harriet Tubman in Dorchester County and Fredrick Douglass in Talbot County. In addition, the Eastern Shore is home to the oldest black community in the country, the Hill neighborhood in Easton, Maryland. The Hill neighborhood dates back to 1787 when a free blackman by the name of James Freeman moved there. Three years later, there were more than 400 free blacks living in the community.

The rich history and the rich farmland provide ample reasons for scientists to continue searching for a solution to save the Eastern Shore. Farming has changed over the centuries on the peninsula, but the need for food to eat is only expanding as the population explodes. Hopefully, they will find some answers before all is lost.

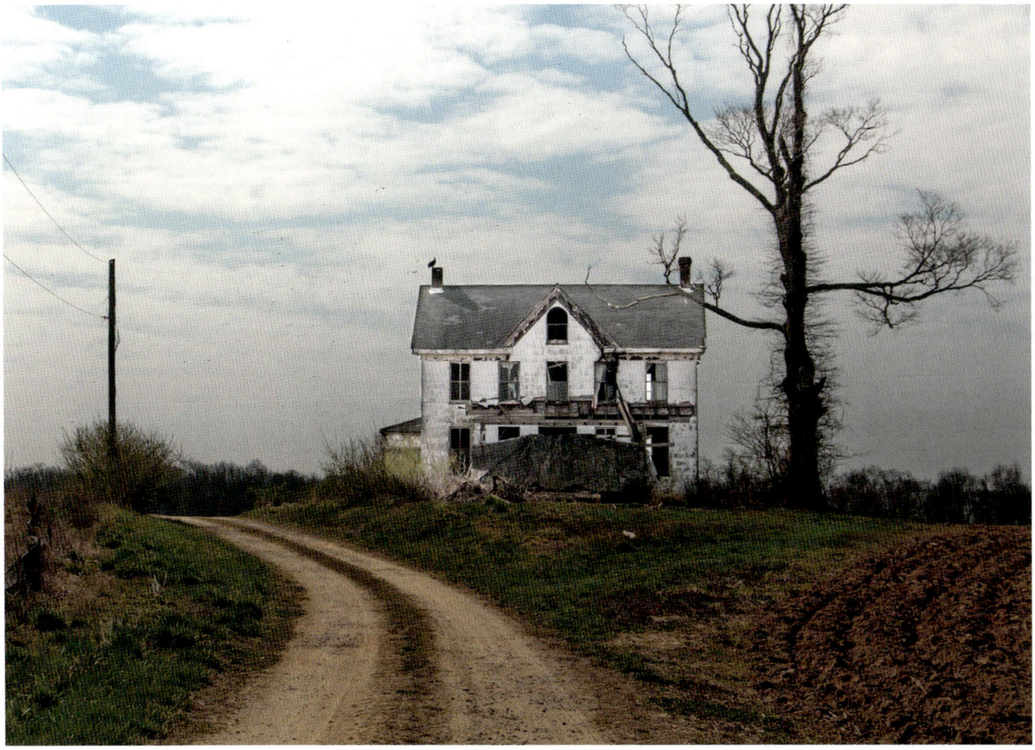

A shell of a farmhouse rotting in the Eastern Shore. [*Robyn*]

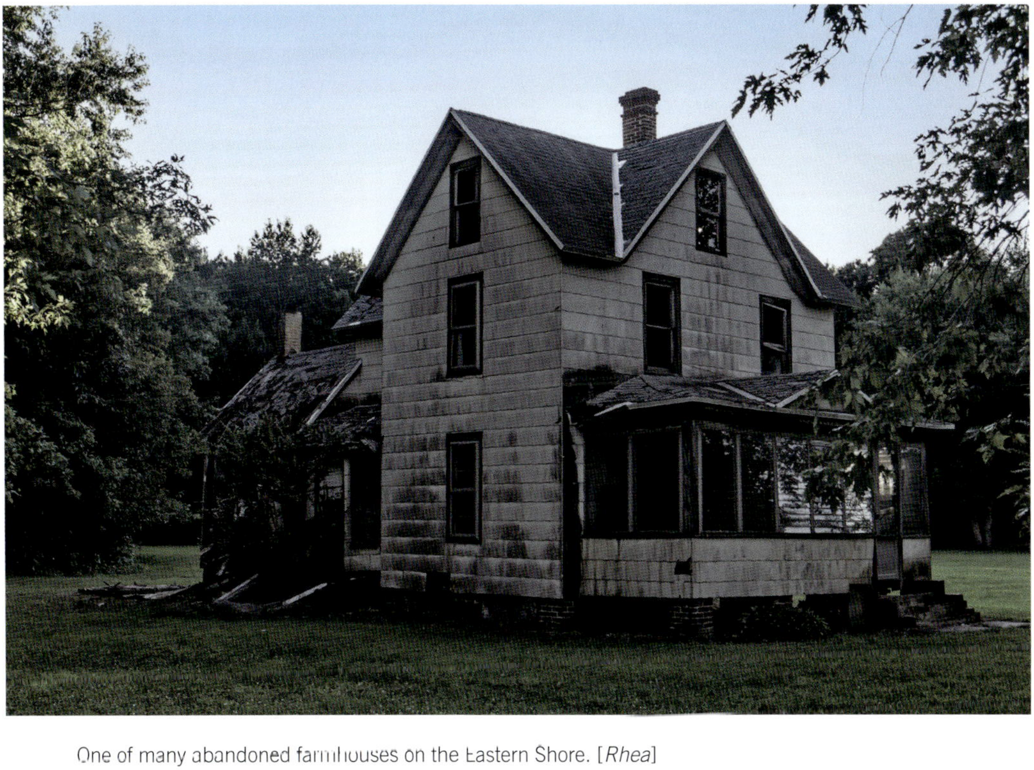

One of many abandoned farmhouses on the Eastern Shore. [*Rhea*]

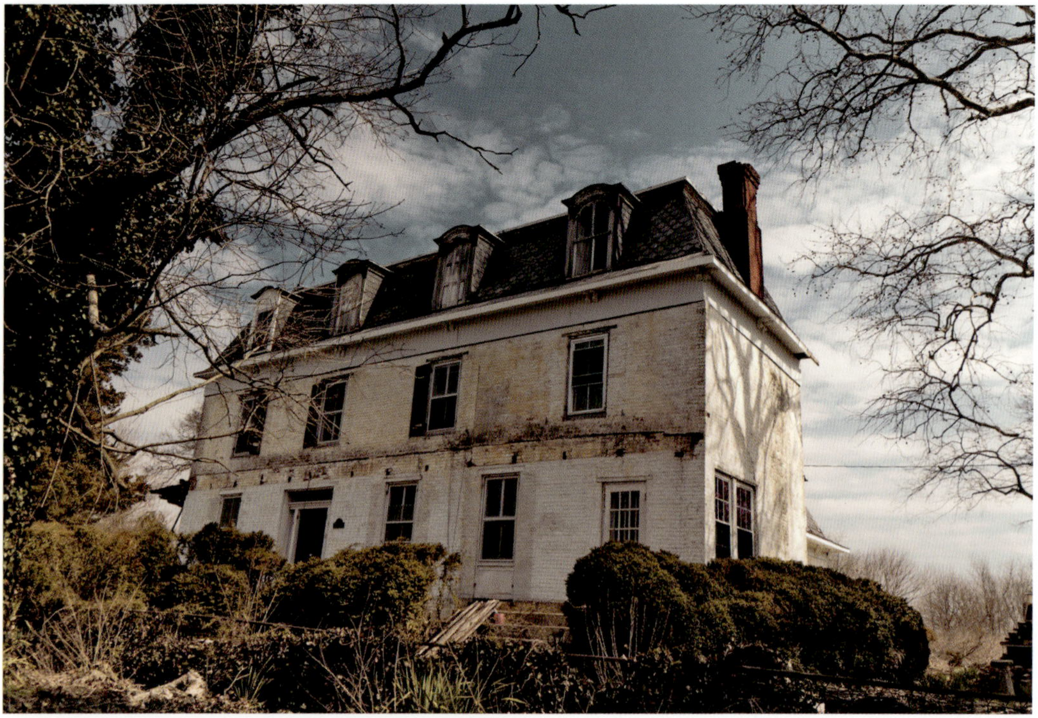

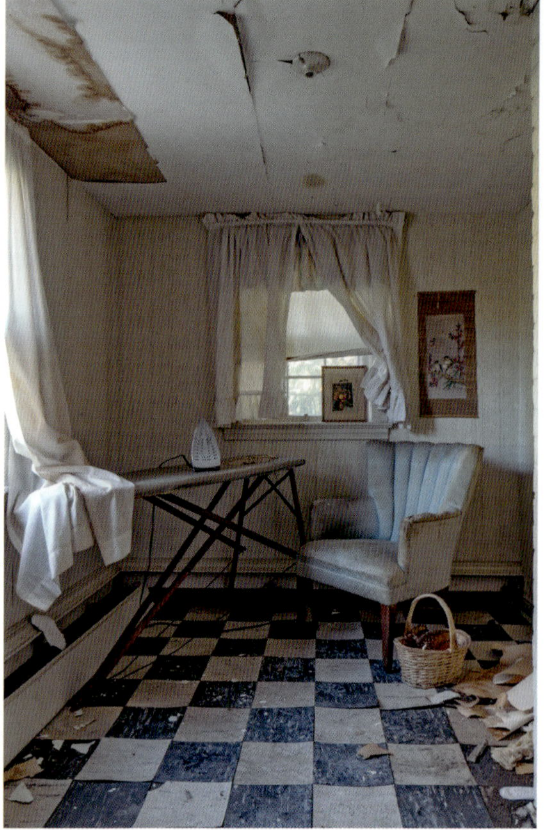

Above: An Eastern Shore historic Second Empire manor that appears to have undergone an attempt at renovation. [*Rhea*]

Left: Items left inside a Victorian home on the Eastern shore. [*Rhea*]

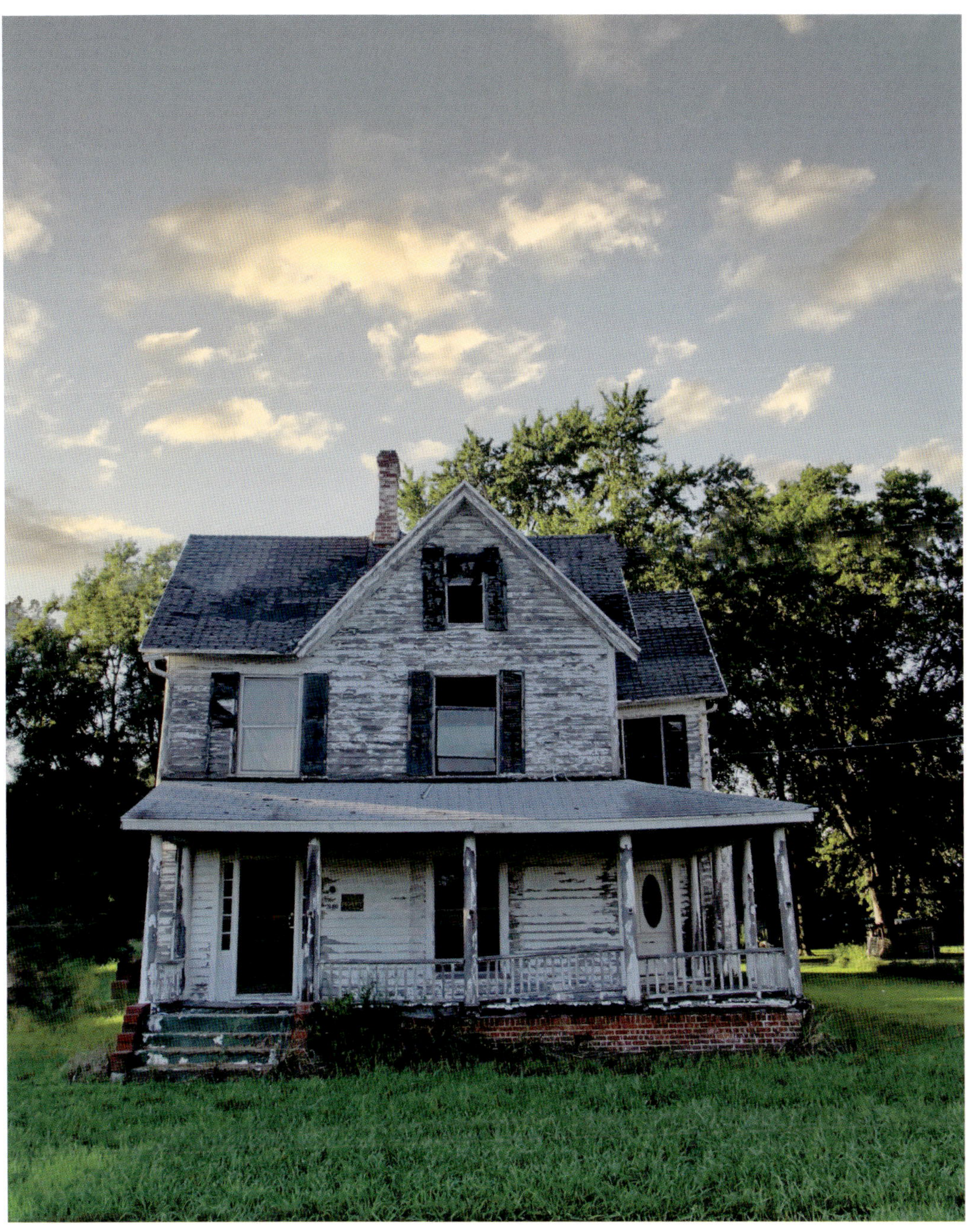

One of the many historic homes left decaying to time on the Eastern shore. [*Robyn*]

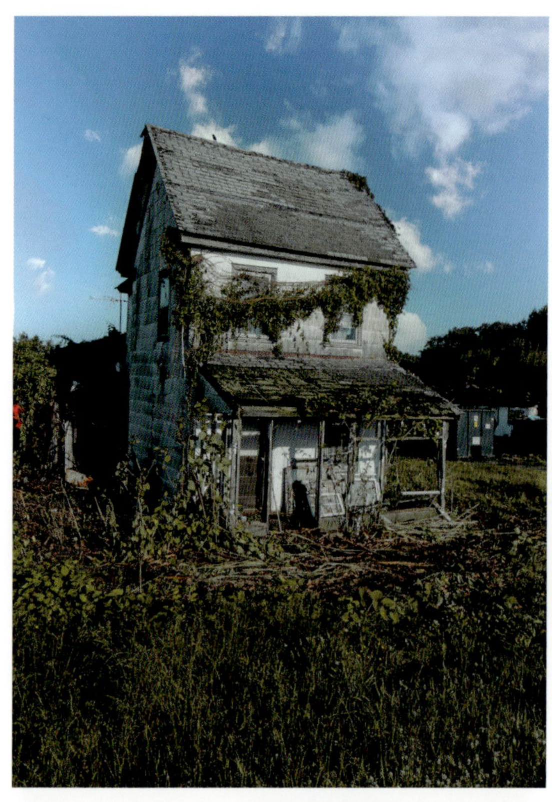

An abandoned home on the shore, also called the Delmarva region, haunts passersby. [*Robyn*]

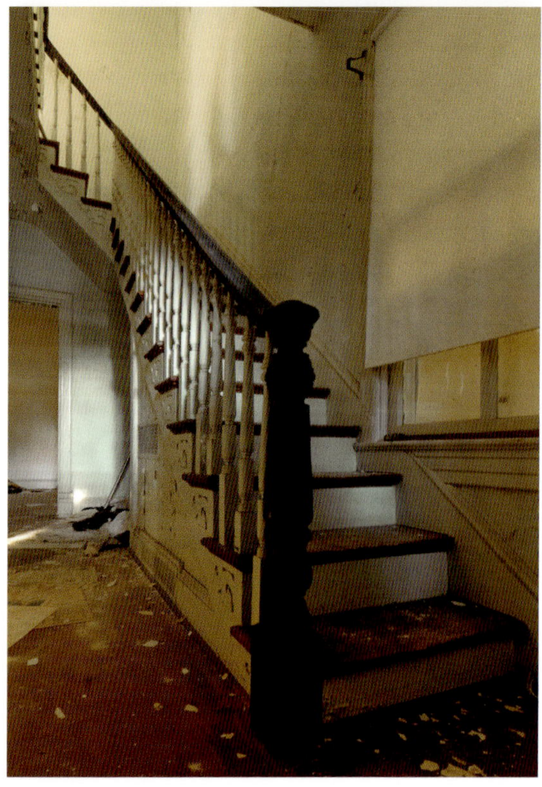

Stairs crumble with time inside a Victorian home on the Eastern shore. [*Robyn*].

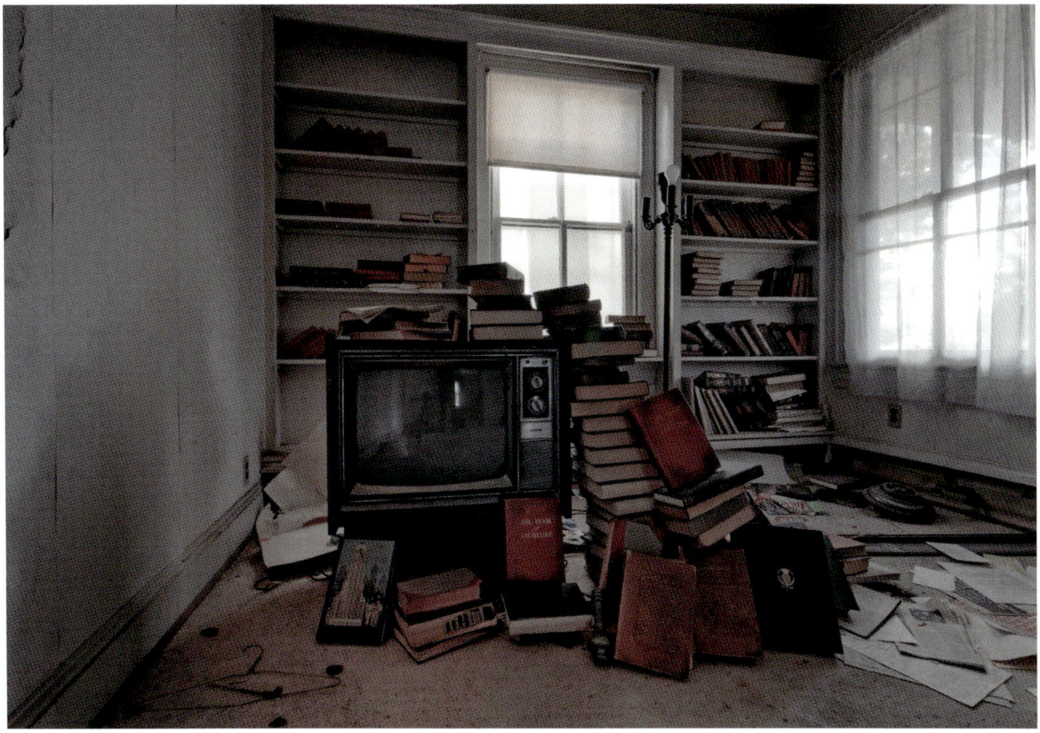

A vintage TV and books that were arranged by a previous explorer inside an Eastern shore home. [*Robyn*]

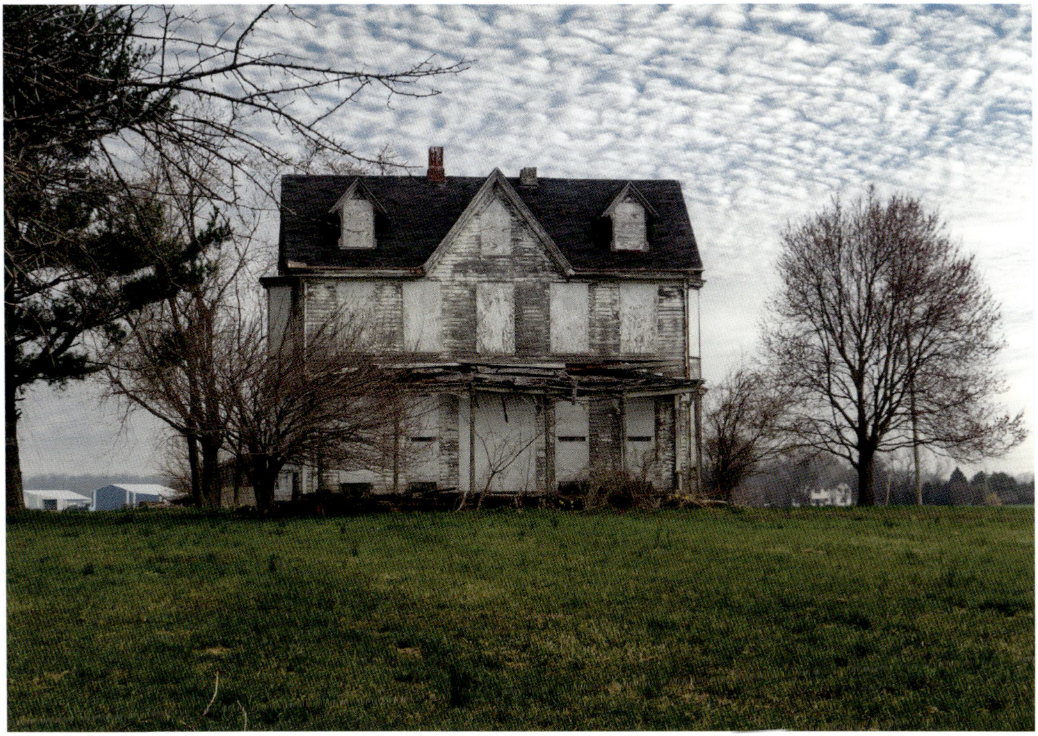

One of many boarded abandoned farms that exist on the Eastern Shore. [*Rhea*]

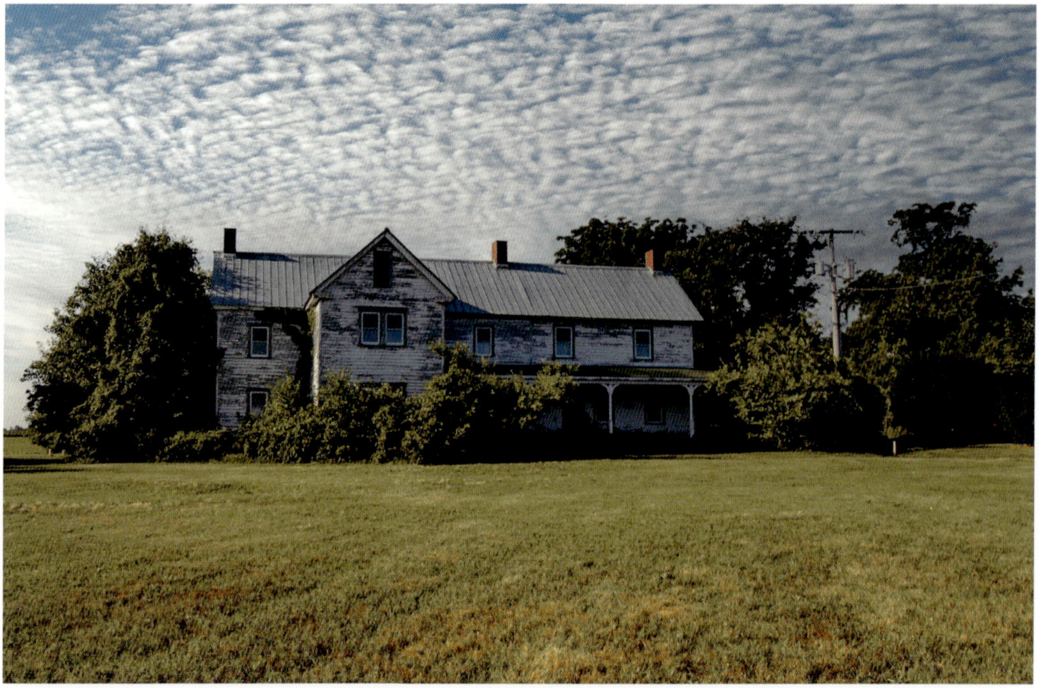

A late nineteenth-century Victorian-era farm decays on the Eastern Shore. [*Robyn*]

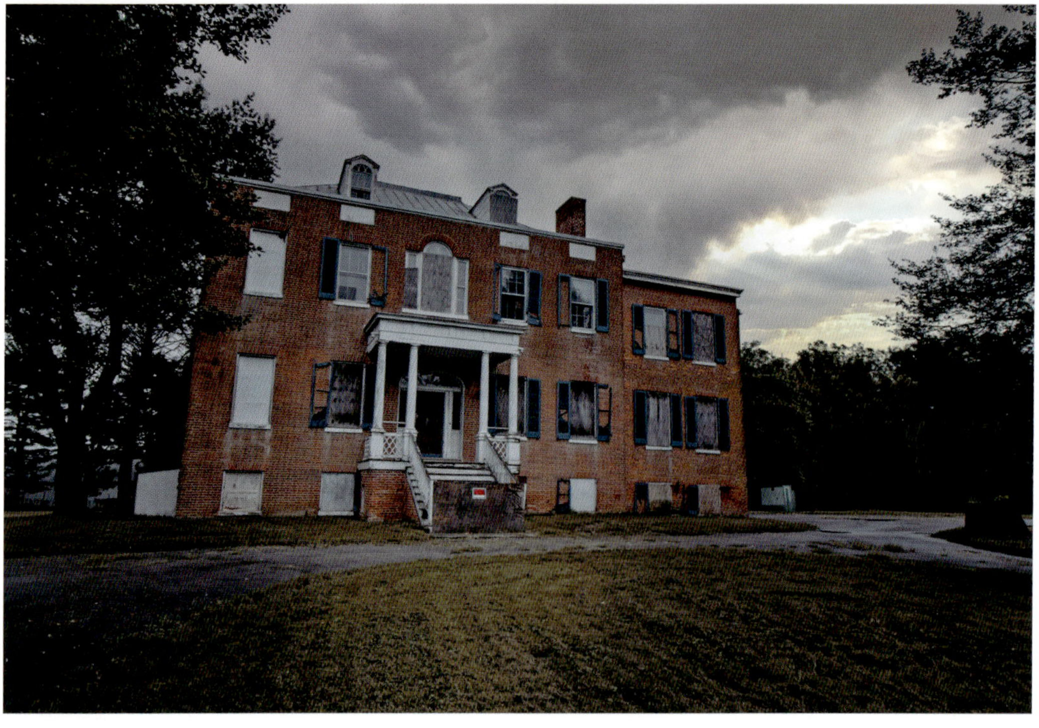

Originally on 225 acres of land, this heavily boarded federal-style mansion was built more than 200 years ago and is on the National Register of Historic Places. This has not prevented its state from falling into utter desperation. [*Robyn*]

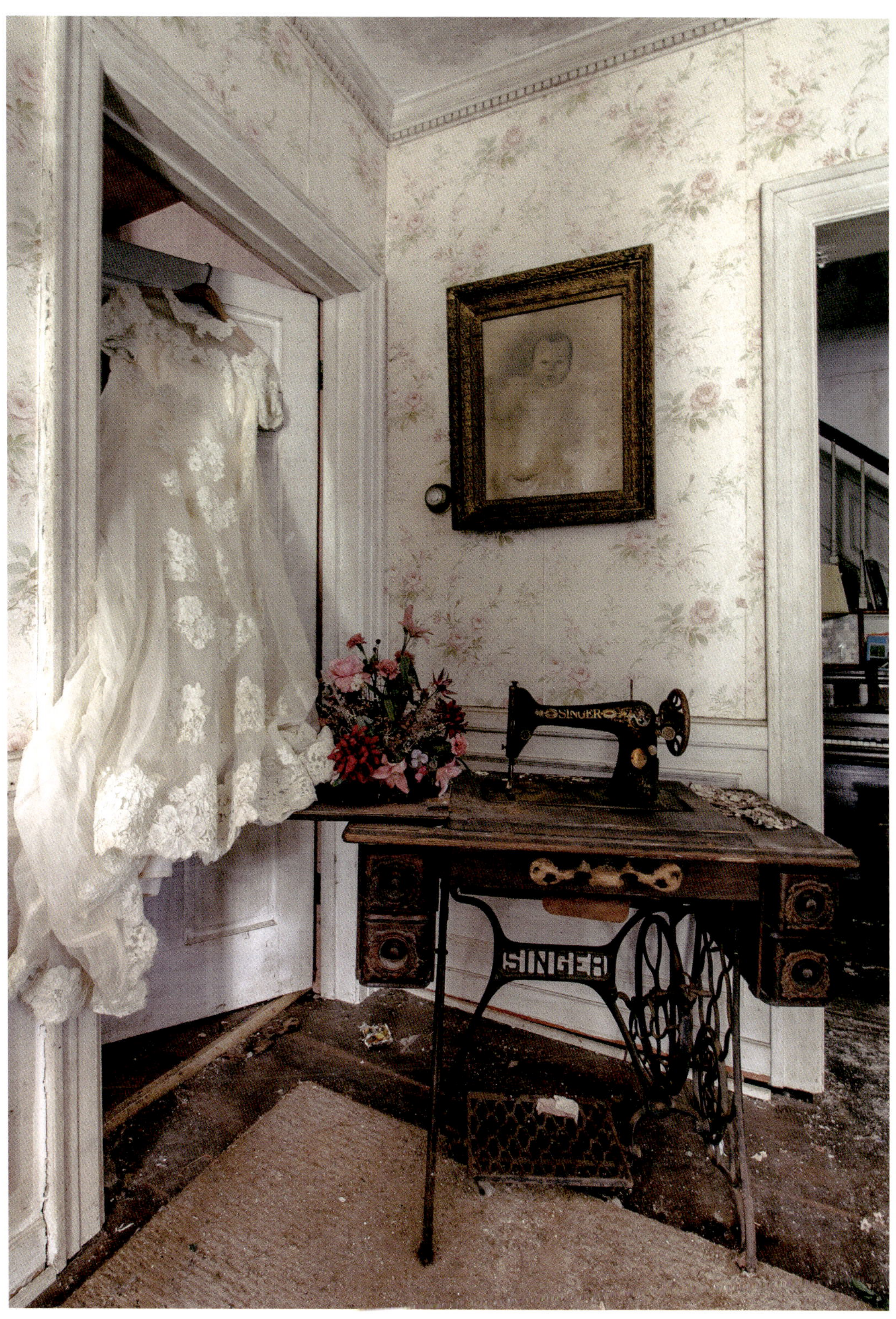

A vintage wedding dress, antique manual treadle, Singer sewing machine, and black-and-white baby portrait are among the many relics left behind in this abandoned farmhouse. [*Rhea*]

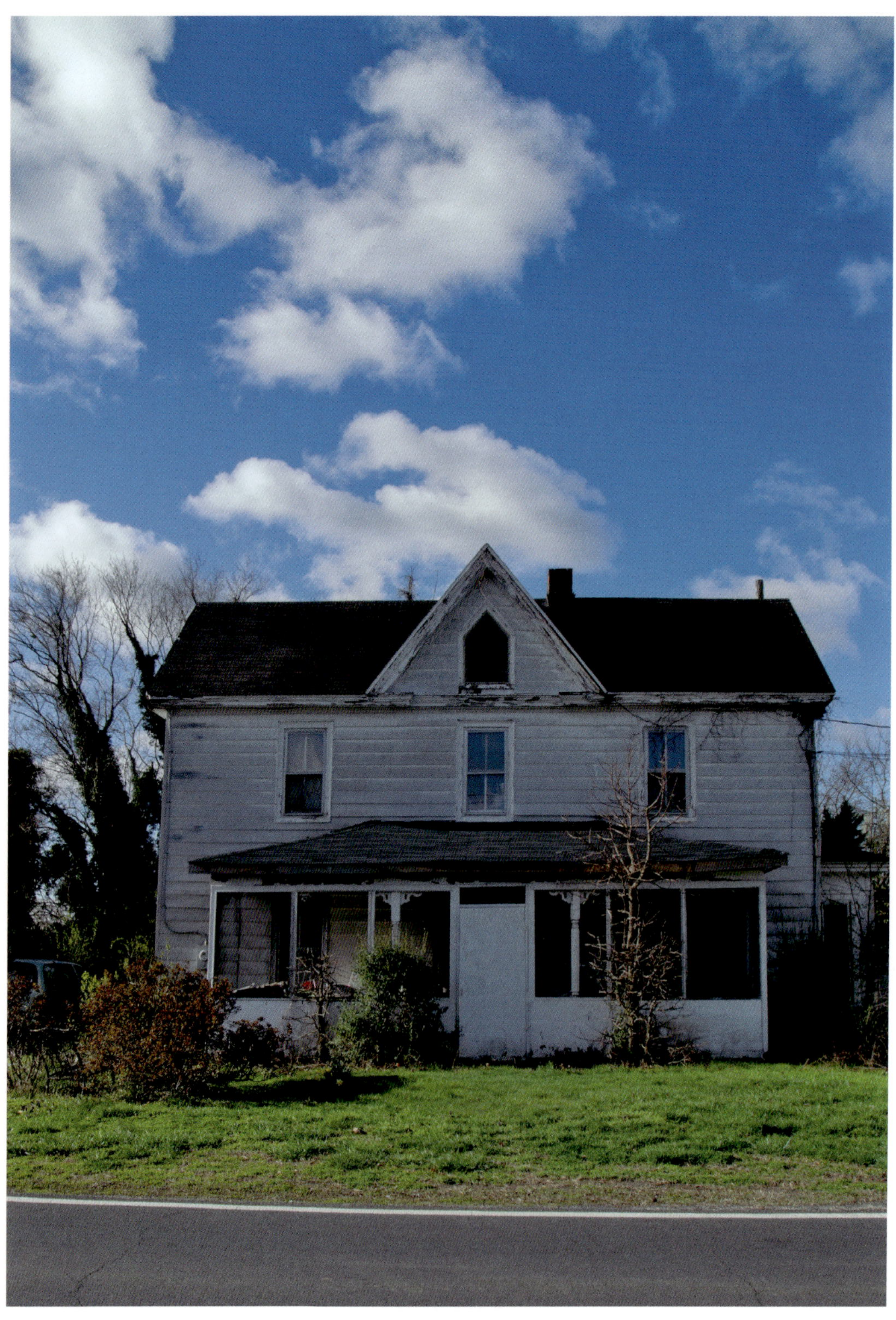

Another dilapidated Folk Victorian on the Eastern shore. [*Robyn*]

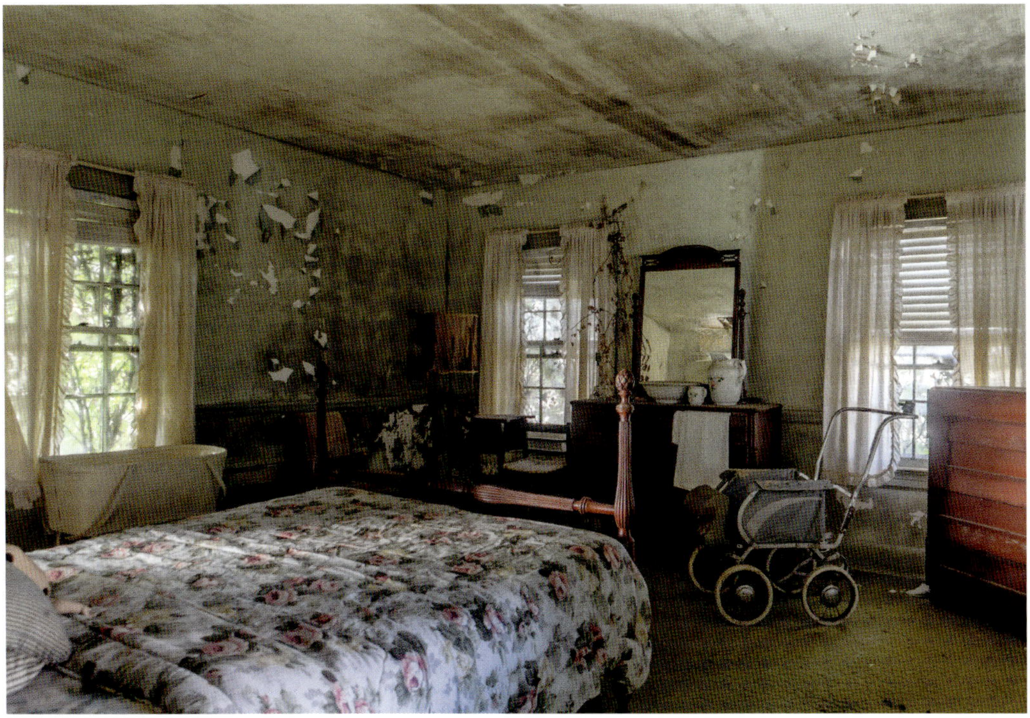

A mid-century baby carriage and antiques inside an abandoned farmhouse. [*Rhea*]

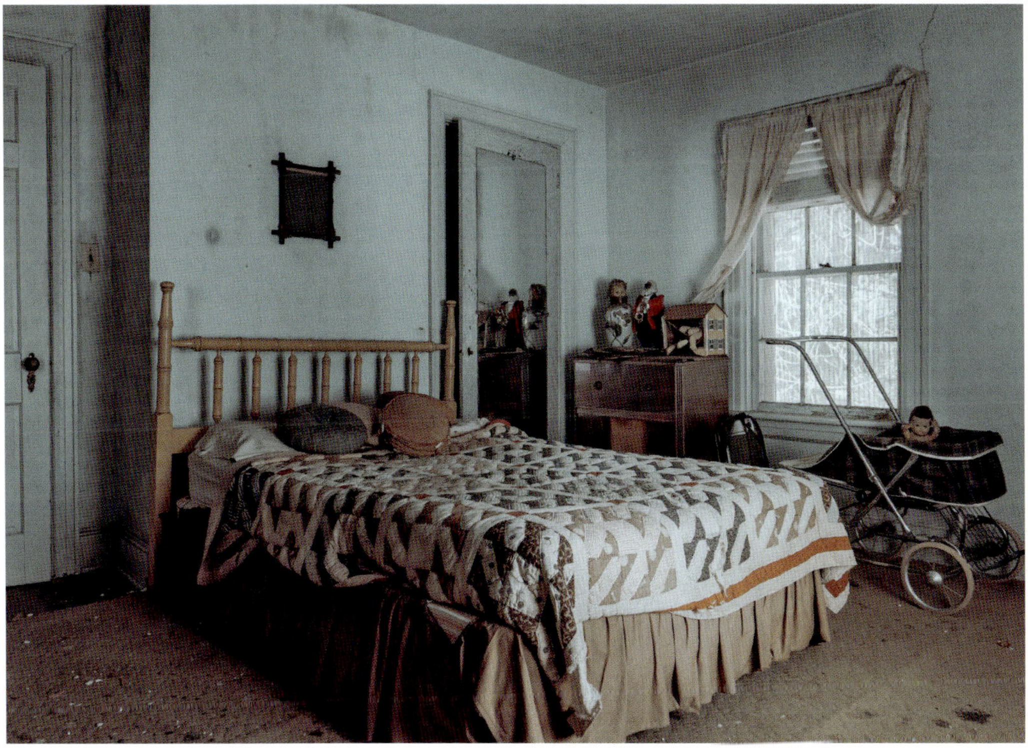

A mid-twentieth-century baby carriage inside an abandoned farm. [*Rhea*]

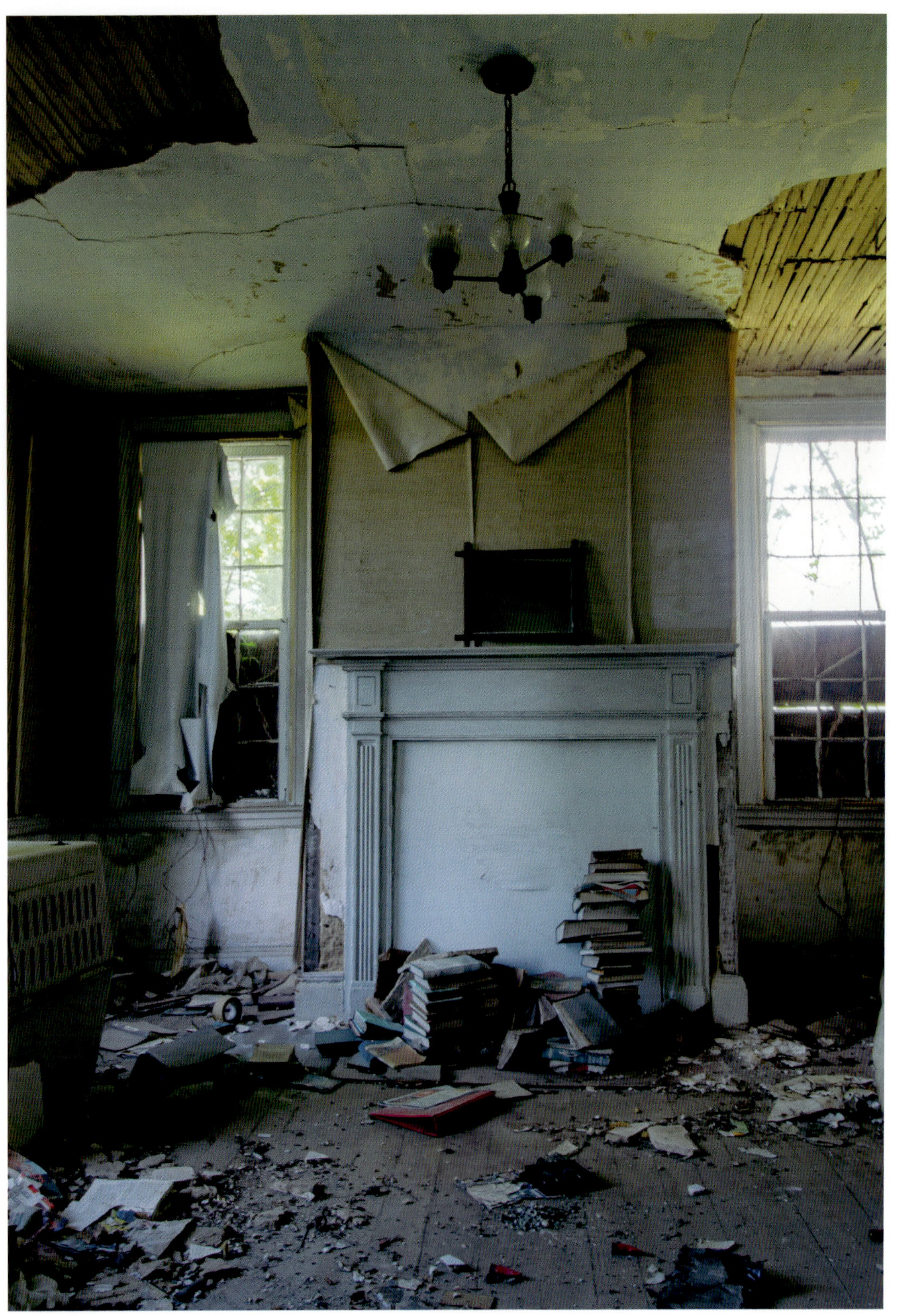

Books are piled in the parlor of a Colonial-style home on the Eastern shore. [*Rhea*]

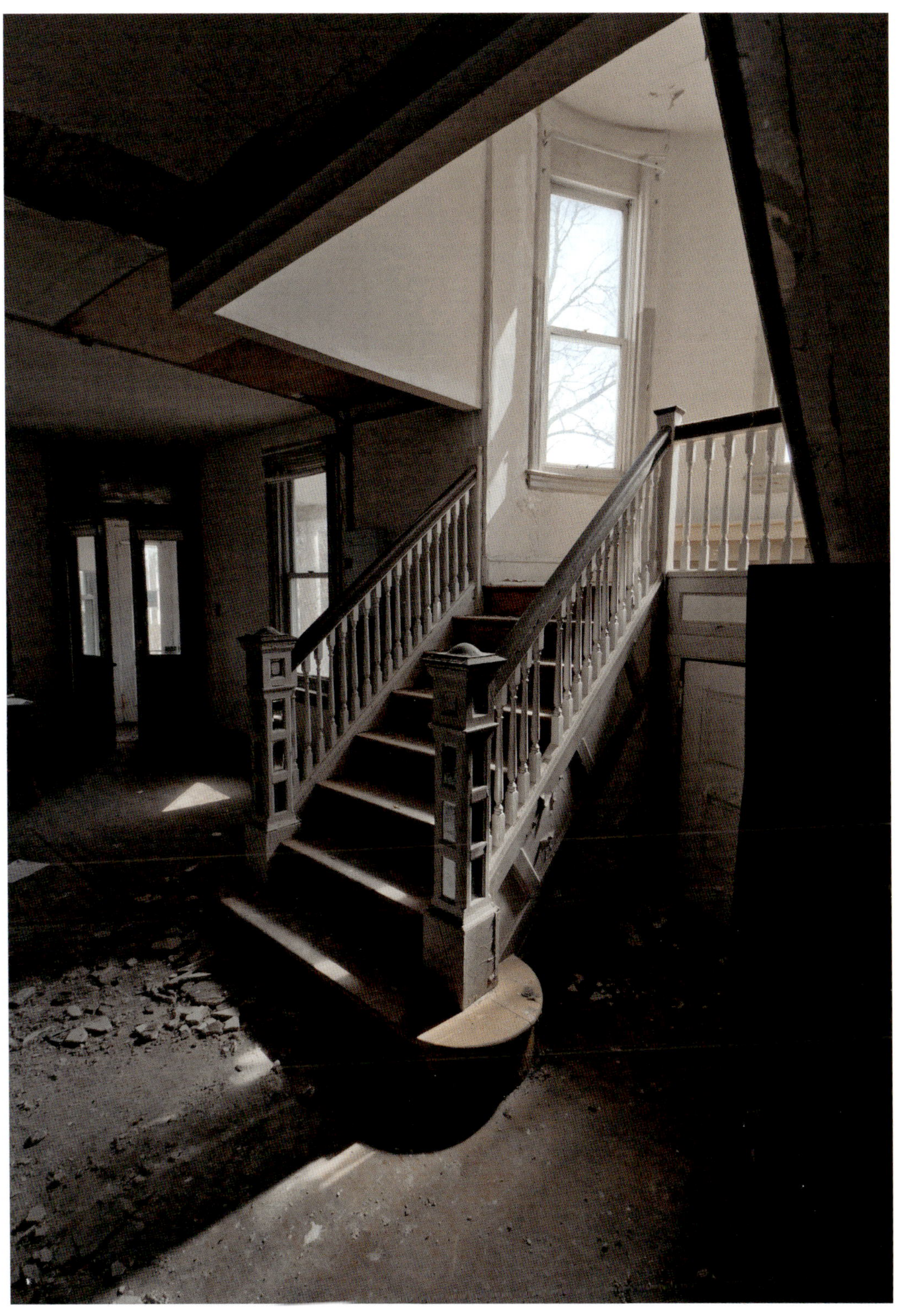

The staircase of a Second Empire mansion that contains an ominous past. The family vanished mysteriously. [*Robyn*]

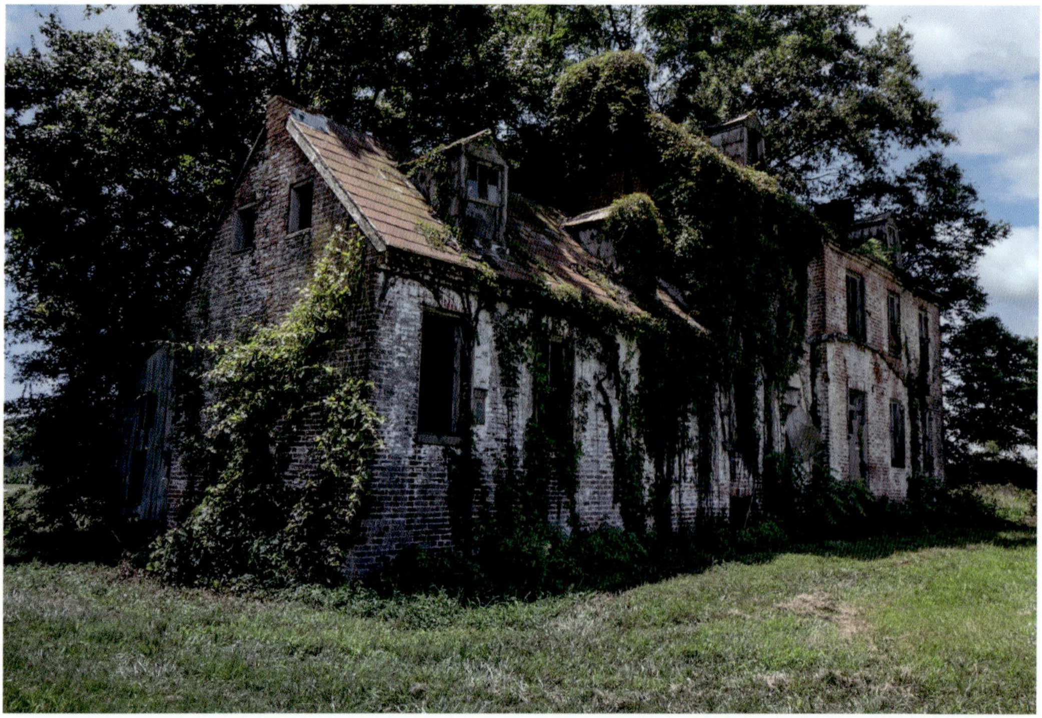

Another Tidewater region relic, this brick manor was built in two parts, first in 1815 and expanded in 1829. Its shell appears as if it has been consumed with fire. [*Rhea*]

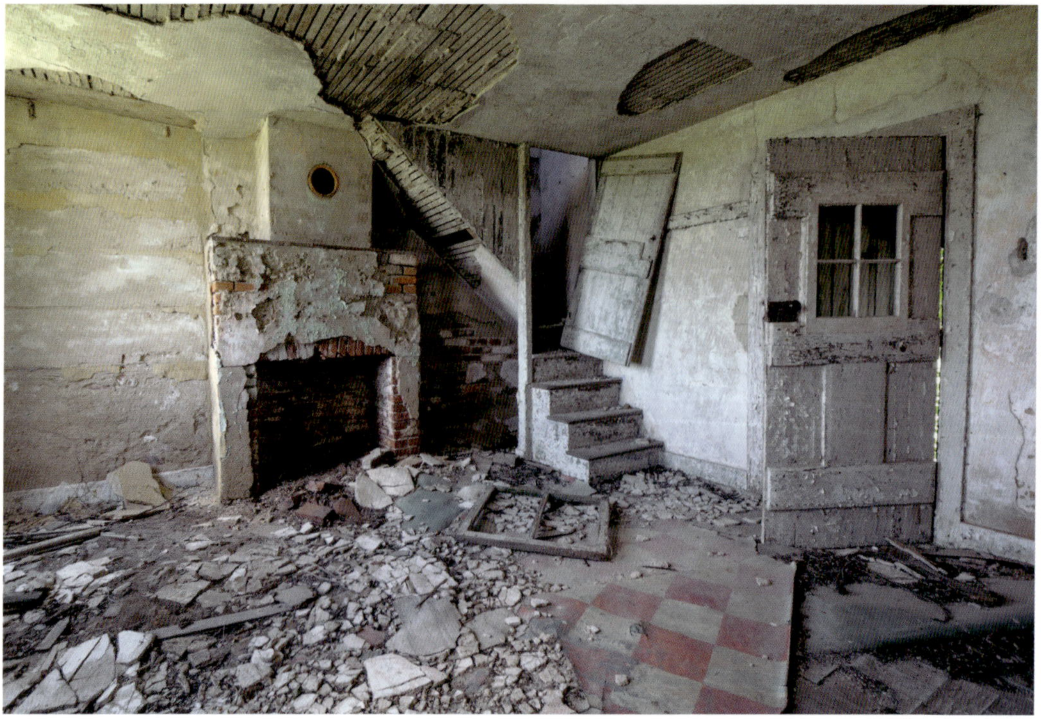

The burned living room of the Tidewater region manor on the Eastern Shore. [*Rhea*]

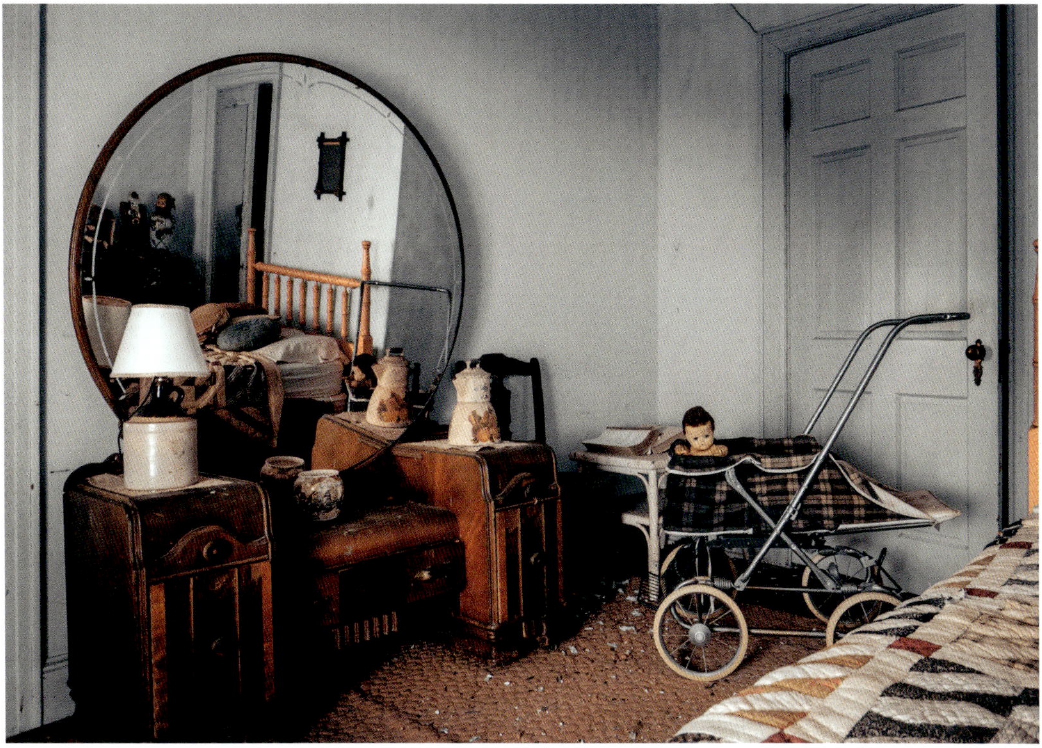

An Art Deco vanity table left in an abandoned farmhouse. [*Rhea*]

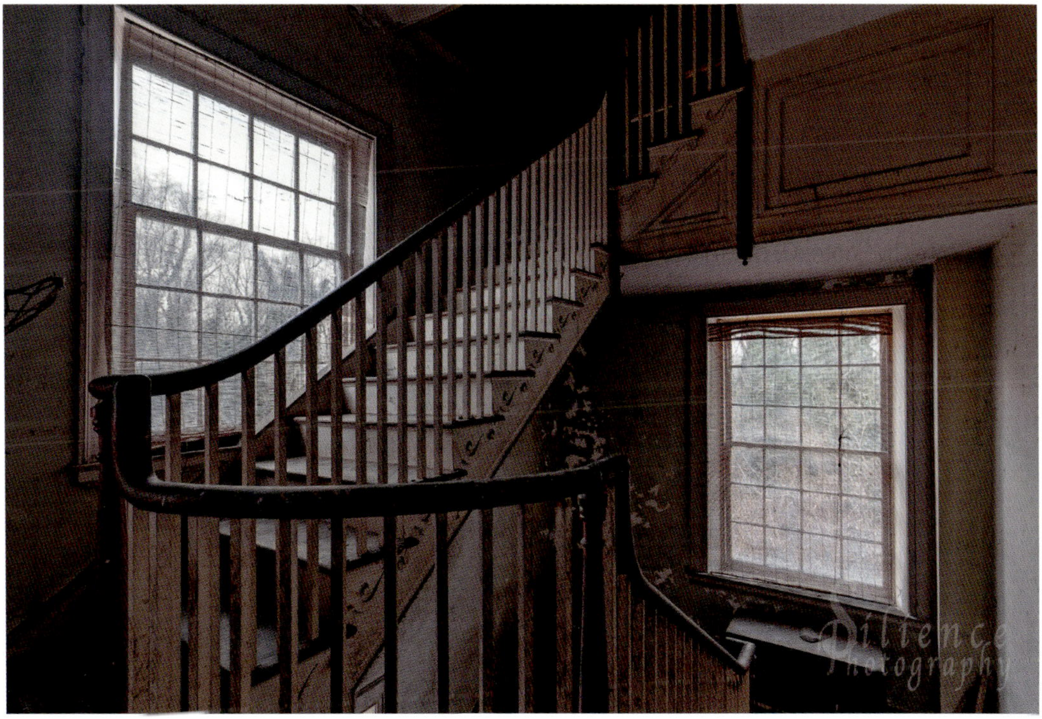

Stairs that lead to the attic in an Eastern Shore plantation. [*Rhea*]

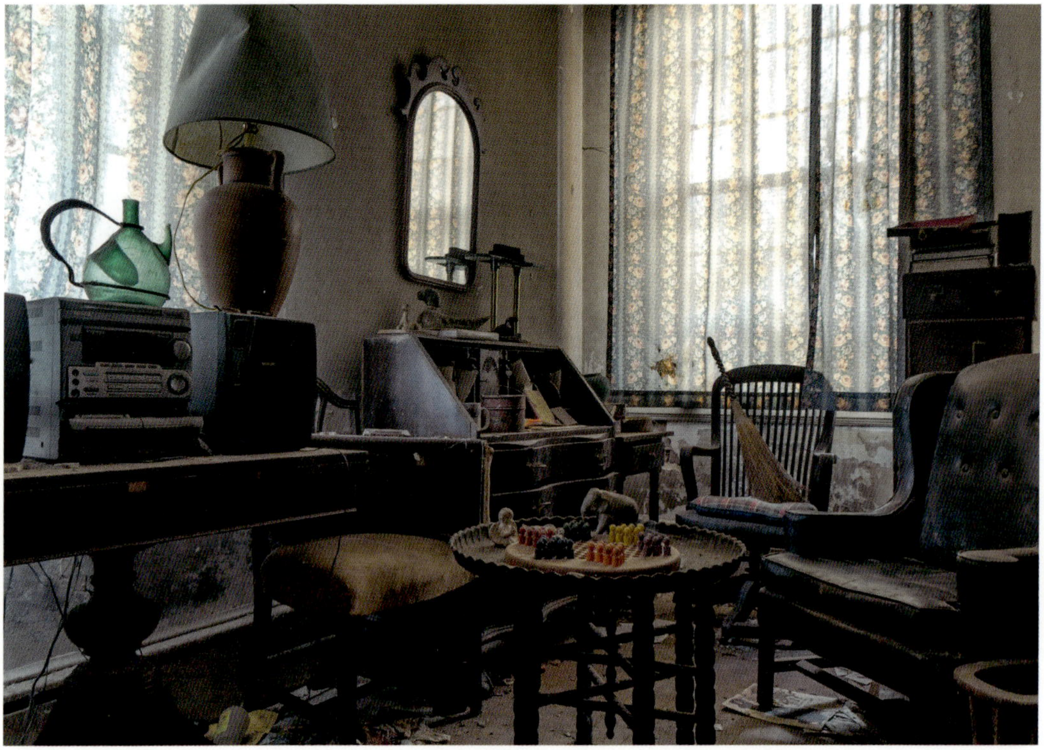

A historic Colonial-era plantation that bursts with antiques and vintage furniture. [*Rhea*]

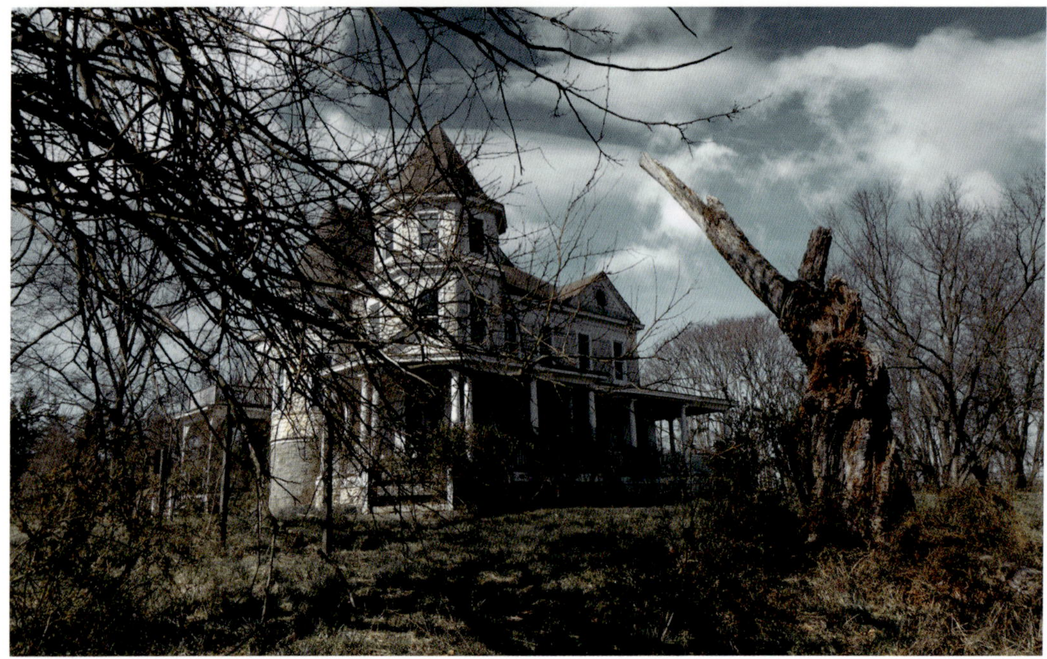

Constructed in 1905, this Second Empire mansion possesses a menacing history. The original family supposedly vanished, and a man who visited the house cited it as one of the reasons he murdered his wife and son and committed suicide, according to a newspaper article. [*Rhea*]

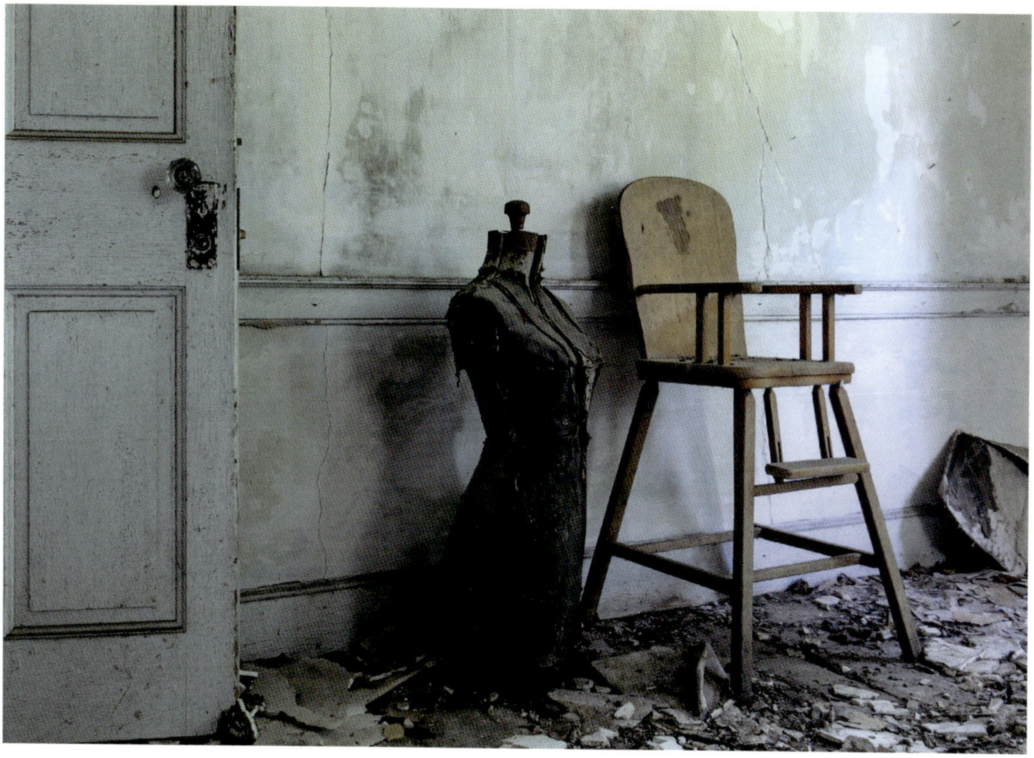

An antique dress form and highchair gather dust inside an eighteenth-century mansion. [*Rhea*]

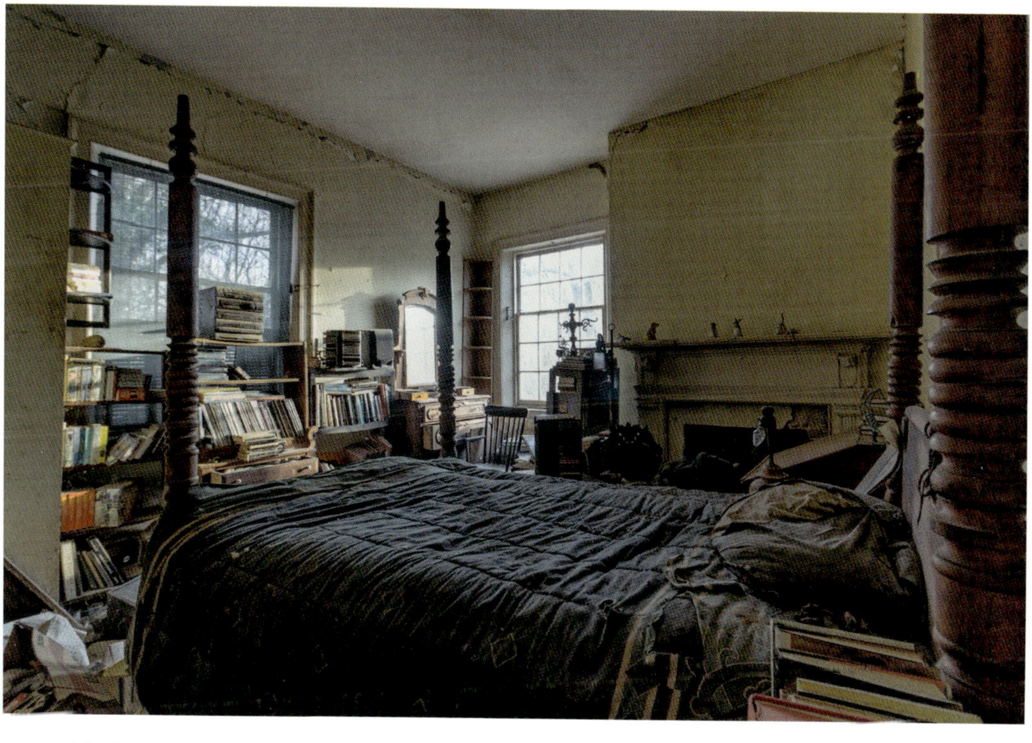

The former owners left antiques piled high in an eighteenth-century mansion. [*Rhea*]

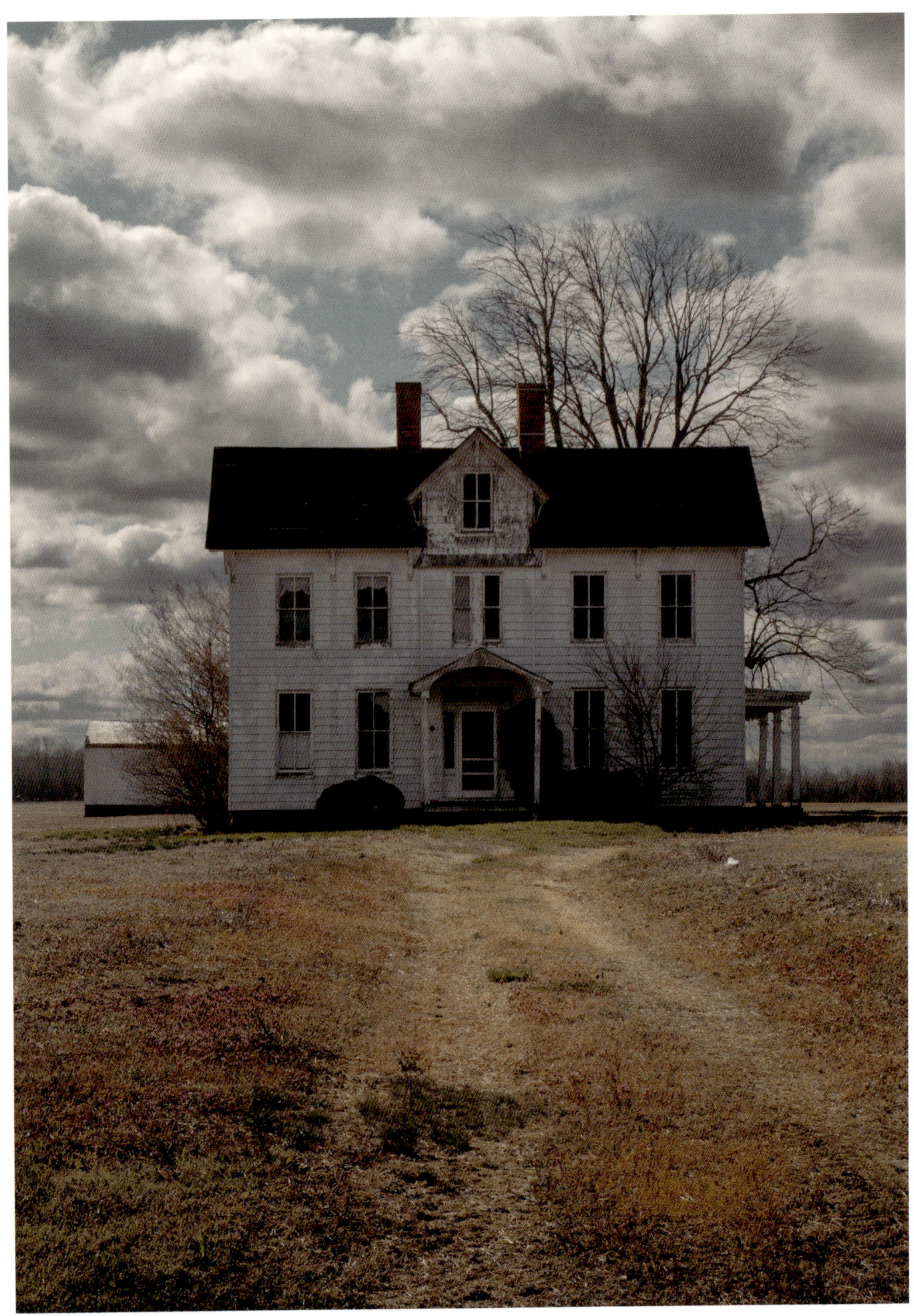

We searched multiple databases and surprisingly could not discover any history on this federal-style plantation on the Eastern Shore. Guessing by other historic farms in the area, we calculate that the house was constructed in the late 1700s or early 1800s. [*Robyn*]

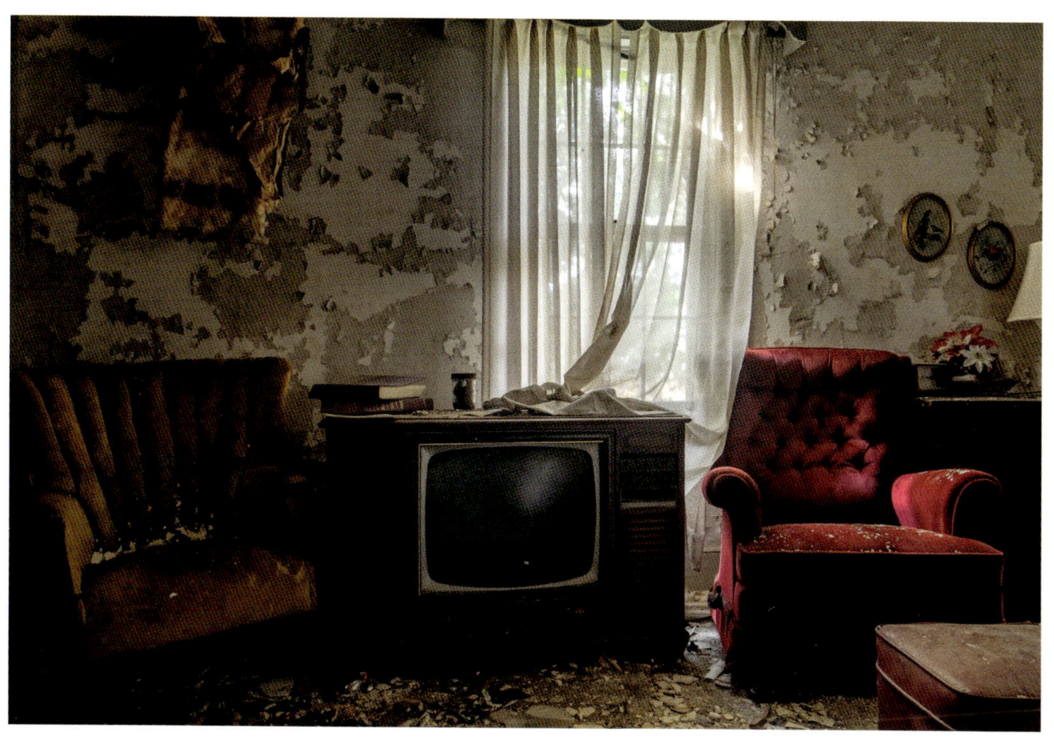

Mid-century chairs and a vintage TV gather dust in an abandoned farm. [*Rhea*]

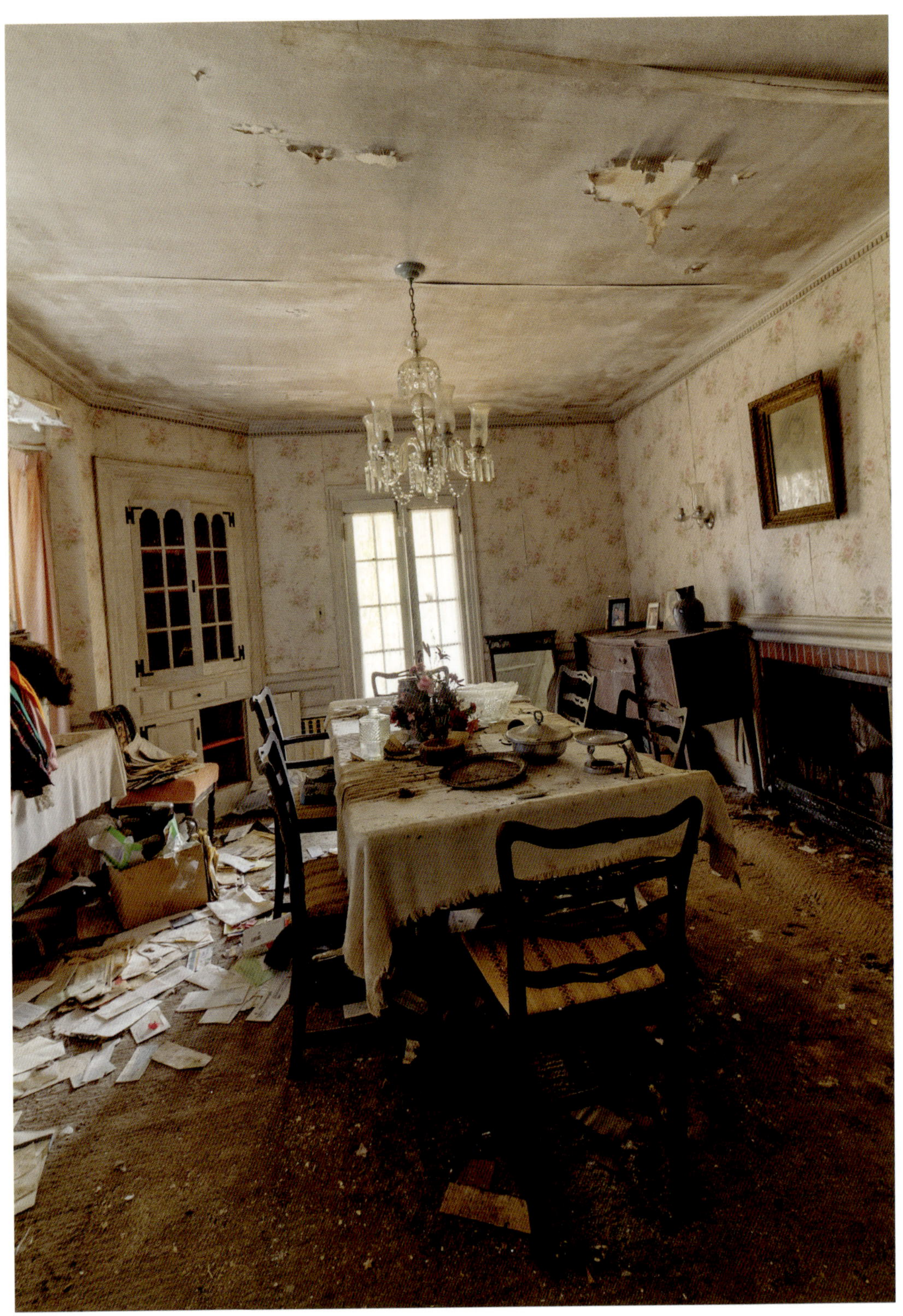

Dishes, antiques, and clothes are among the many personal items that remain inside this farm. [*Robyn*]

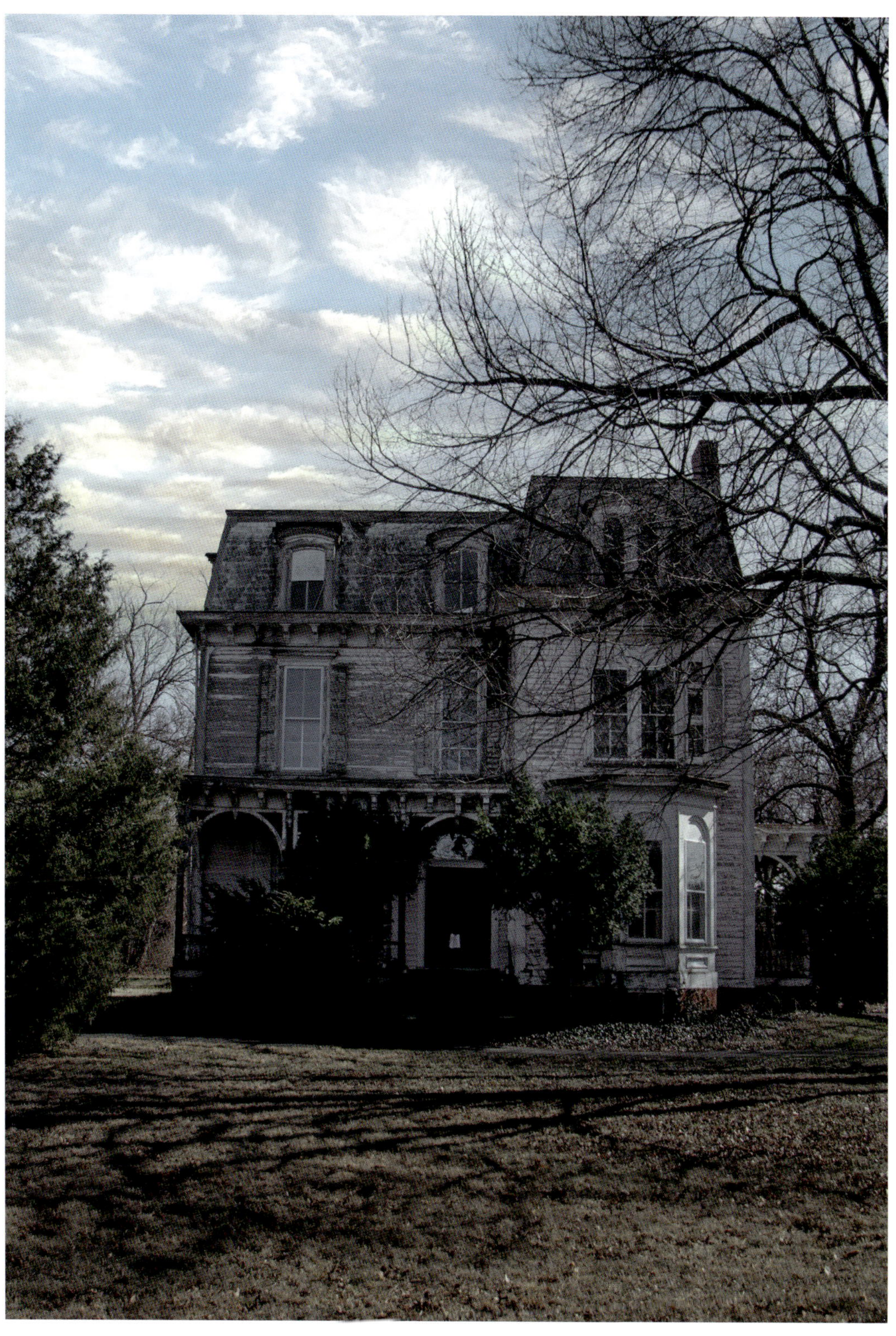

This grand pink Second Empire Victorian was constructed in 1870. The 4,909-square-foot mansion features seven bedrooms, and the exterior boasts intricate architectural finishings. [*Rhea*]

4

STONEWALL FARM

Truly one of our favorite mansions sat tucked at the end of a tree-lined driveway in a historic neighborhood not far from Baltimore. It had four-bedrooms, 5,292 square feet, and was a Second-Empire Victorian. Built in 1808, the earliest proprietors originally built the residence in the federal style of architecture. Later in the century, the owners undertook renovations to transition it to the Second Empire fashion when they added a mansard roof, double-deck porches, polychrome slate, and stucco coating, according to the Maryland Historic Properties website.

The website also suggests that a wealthy Quaker named Benjamin P. Moore retained the home around 1839. Moore (who is not the same Moore as the paint store namesake) had partnered in a grocery business with entrepreneur and philanthropist Johns Hopkins called Hopkins & Moore (the same Hopkins of Johns Hopkins University), a relationship that dissolved in 1813. Moore had married Mary Hopkins in 1797. After Moore's ownership, Thomas Lansdale and then Thomas C. Miller became the manor's proprietors. Both were investors in a cotton factory. Lansdale dubbed the estate "Enfield." In 1875, Mrs. Isabella T. Skinner rechristened it "Stonewall Farm."

In 1986, Stonewall Farm underwent another renovation and received a late twentieth-century kitchen and bathrooms, and the owners installed an indoor pool. The last proprietor was a doctor. Rumors spread that the doctor was placed in a nursing home, leading to the abandonment of the stately manor since the 1990s. Of all the estates we have ever explored, this is among the few that have haunted us, because its demise is a tragic blow to history. Explorers had dubbed it the "pink bedroom" mansion. Upstairs, there was a beautiful little girl's room that contained a canopy bed with pink flowered wallpaper and a pink flowered bedspread. According to urban legend, the doctor, who was a devout Sikh, left the estate to his daughter, and she refused to accept the home. Consequently, it languished unkempt, unlived in, unloved, until someone set it on fire in May 2019, and it disintegrated into ash.

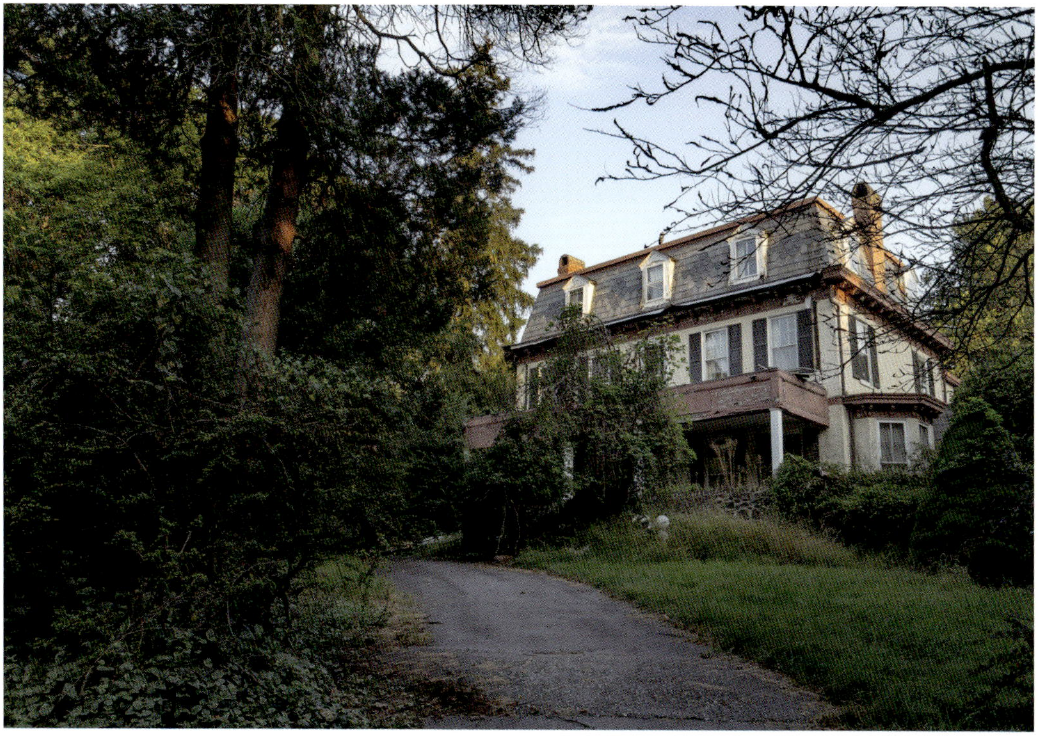

In 2016, the exterior of Stonewall Farm showed decay; a few years later, graffiti covered the facade. [*Robyn*]

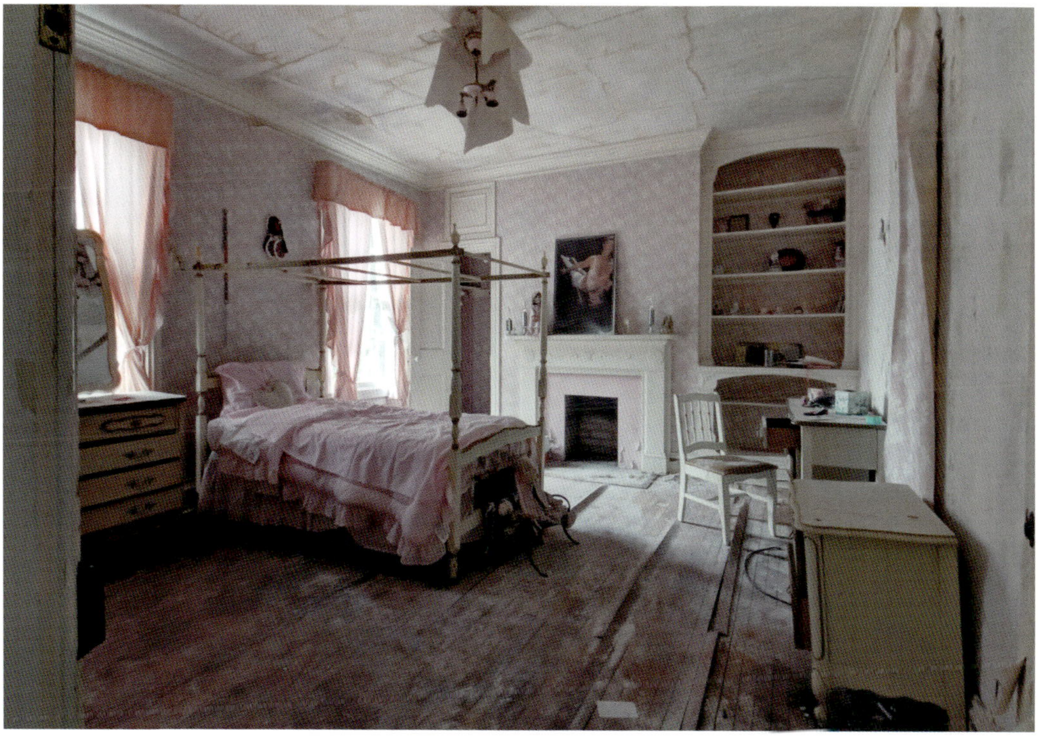

The infamous pink-bedroom inside Stonewall Farm, taken in 2016. Vandals destroyed the canopy by 2017. [*Robyn*]

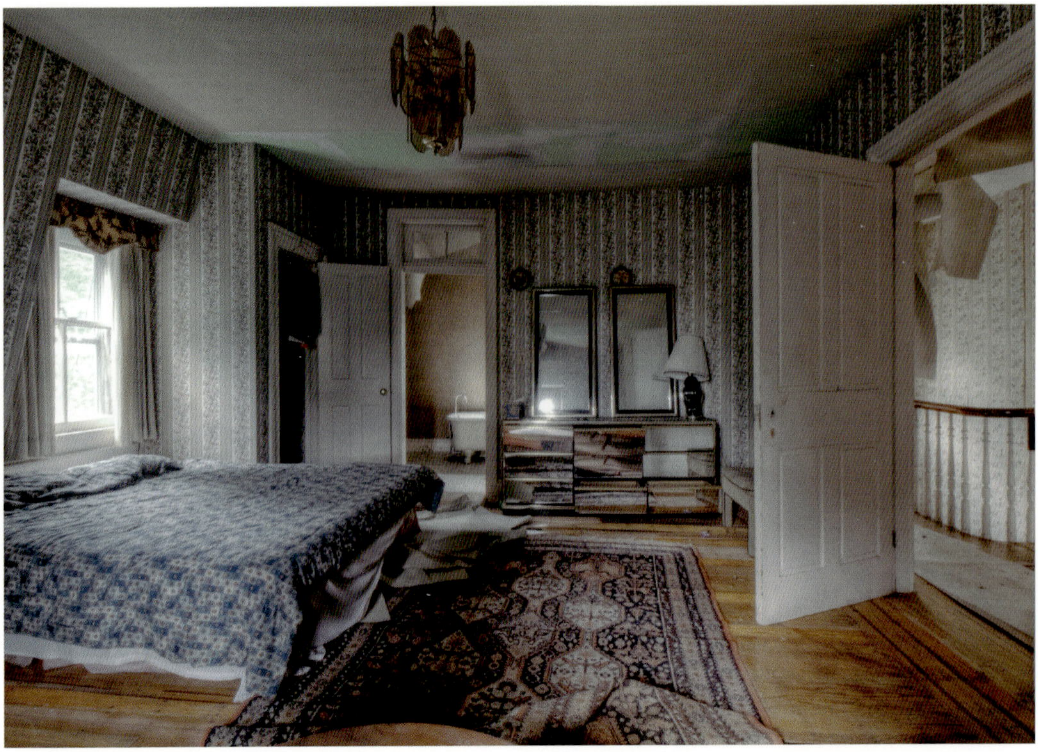

An attic bedroom inside Stonewall Farm that contained an *ensuite* with a bear claw tub. [*Robyn*]

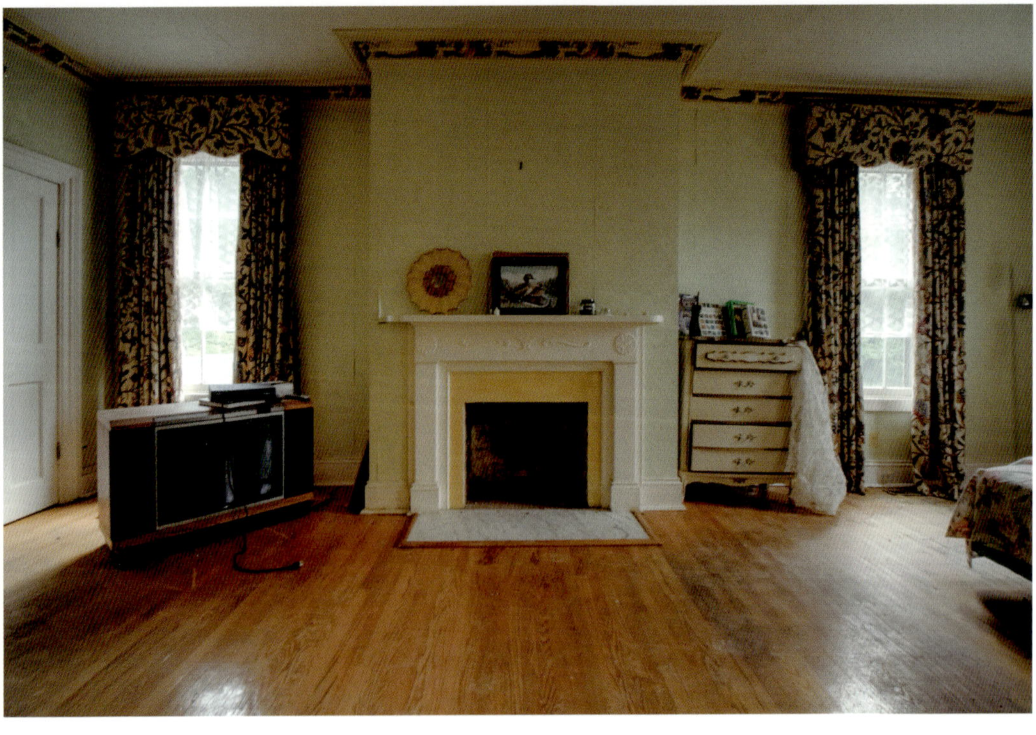

A fireplace inside the master bedroom on the second floor of Stonewall Farm. [*Robyn*]

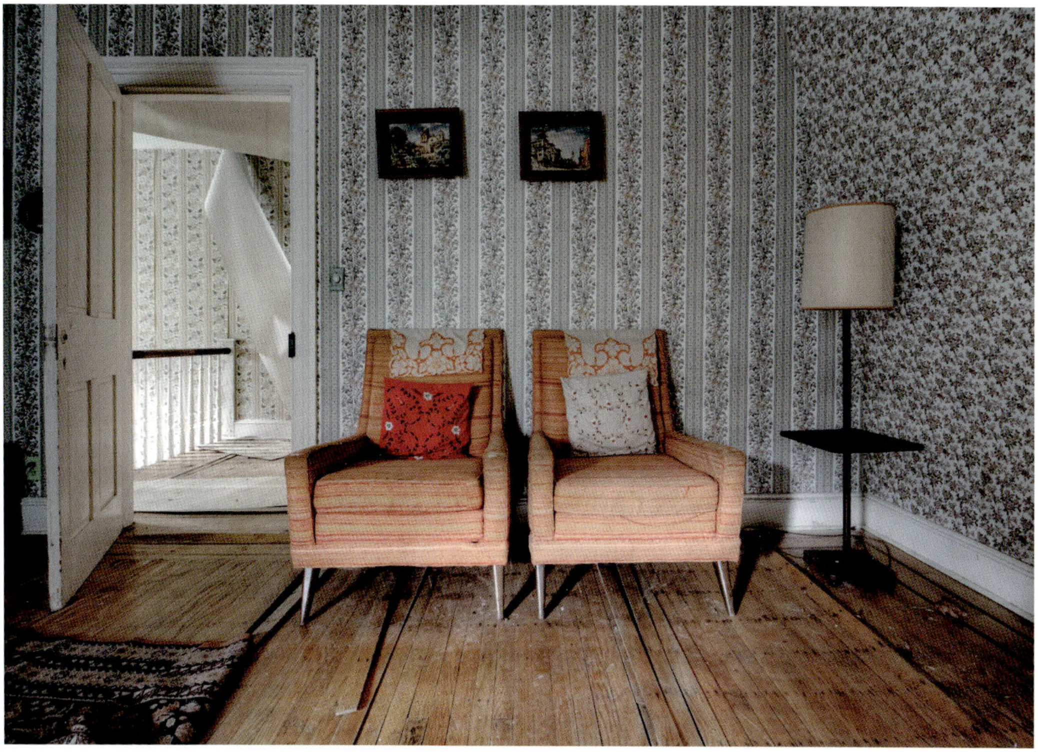

The attic bedroom of Stonewall Farm contained these mid-century modern chairs. [*Robyn*]

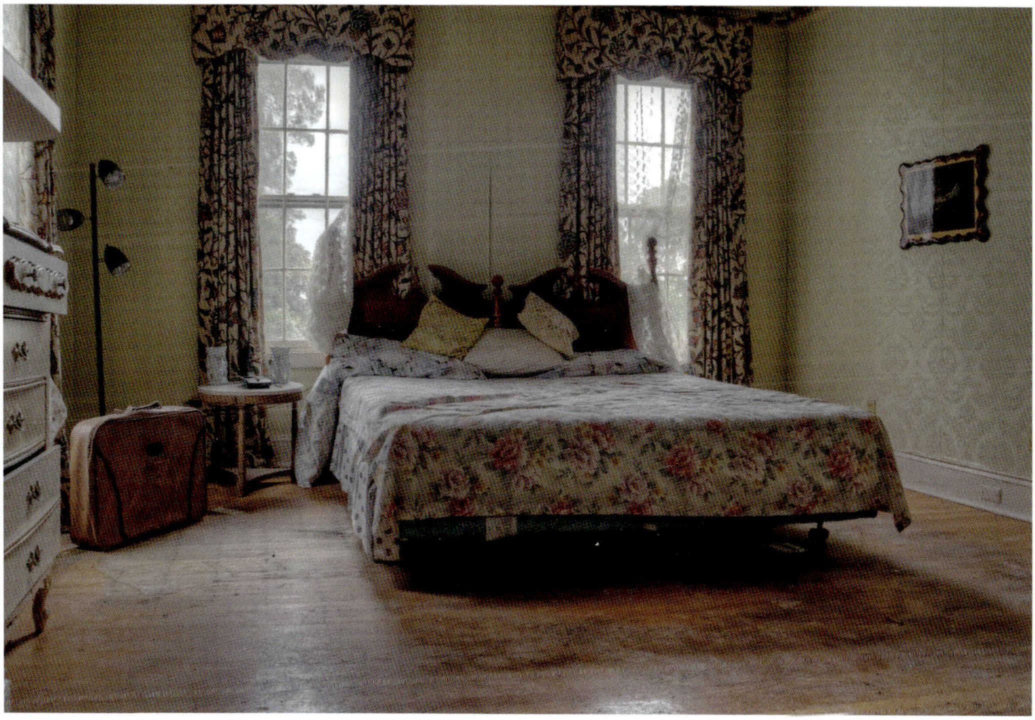

The master suite of Stonewall Farm boasted 1980s decor. [*Robyn*]

5

WINDERBOURNE: VICTORIAN MANSION

Sadness lingers over Winderbourne Mansion, once the summer sojourn of a Washington, D.C., elite couple and a member of the National Register of Historic Places. The Queen-Anne style home was constructed in 1884 and sits on nine acres by the water in rural Maryland. The home's original proprietors were Enoch and Mary Totten. Enoch was a Union Civil War Colonel with the Wisconsin Regiment and a D.C. lawyer. Mary Totten's father was a Wisconsin senator, Timothy Howe, and "the heir of Elias Howe who perfected the sewing machine," according to a 2016 *Washington Post* article. During the Civil War, Enoch survived being shot four times during the Battle of Spotsylvania Courthouse.

Tragedy haunts the mansion as all three of the couple's children contracted typhoid in the house, and one died from illness. The couple's granddaughter, their daughter Edith's child, died after sliding off the stairwell banister. Edith, who became a doctor, died in the home at the age of forty-eight, dropping dead after delivering a lecture at Johns Hopkins University.

The Pickrell family bought the house in 1929. Edward Pickrell was a police officer with the railroad. His son Edward Pickrell Jr. inherited the house and lived there until his death in 2004. For years, his brother Paxton tried to sell the house with no luck. The county bought up much of the land around it to create a park, while the house has languished unlived in for a few decades, falling apart. However, as of 2021, someone has expressed interest in buying and saving Winderbourne, according to an updated *Post* article. Hopefully, this new owner breathes new life into the mansion that has now been scarred by graffiti and vandals.

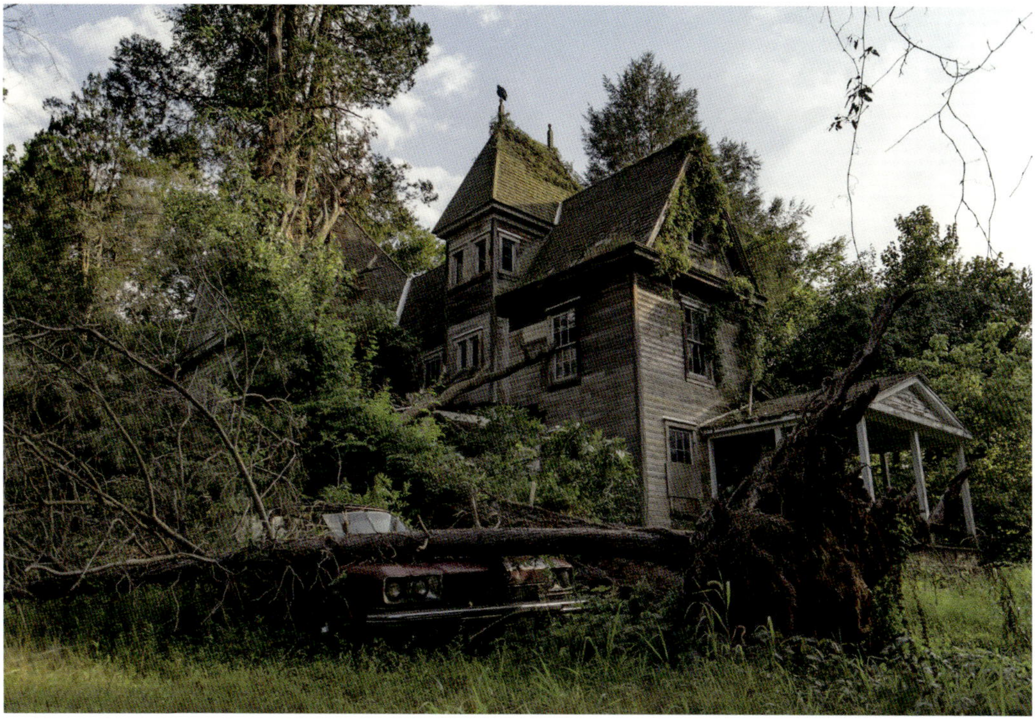

The exterior of a Queen Anne mansion built in 1884. [*Rhea*]

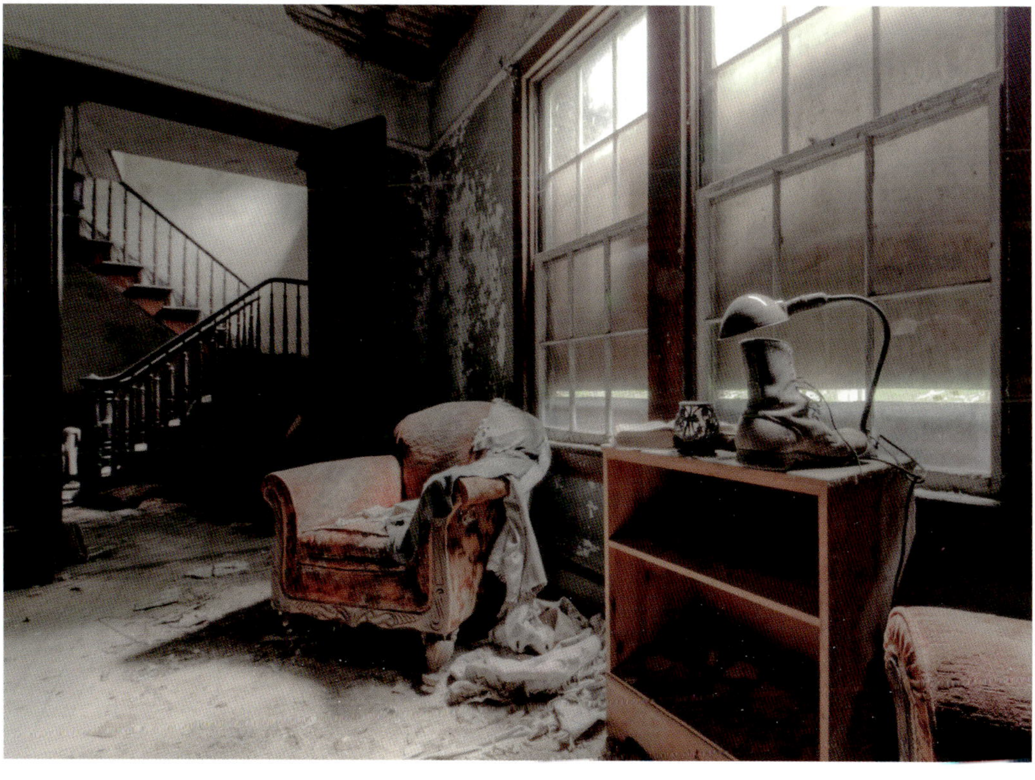

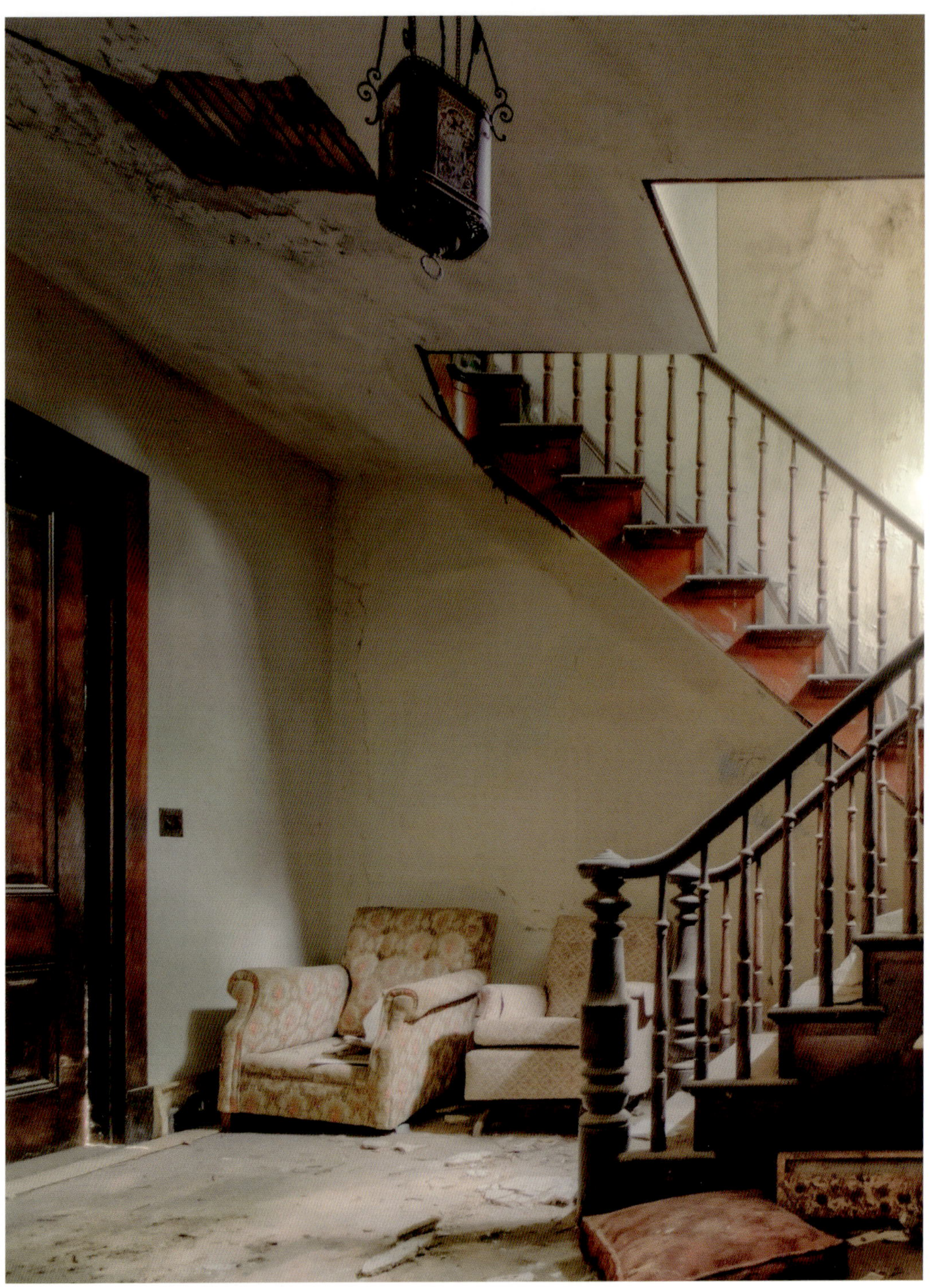

These photos show various scenes from inside this historic Queen Anne mansion. [*Robyn* and *Rhea*]

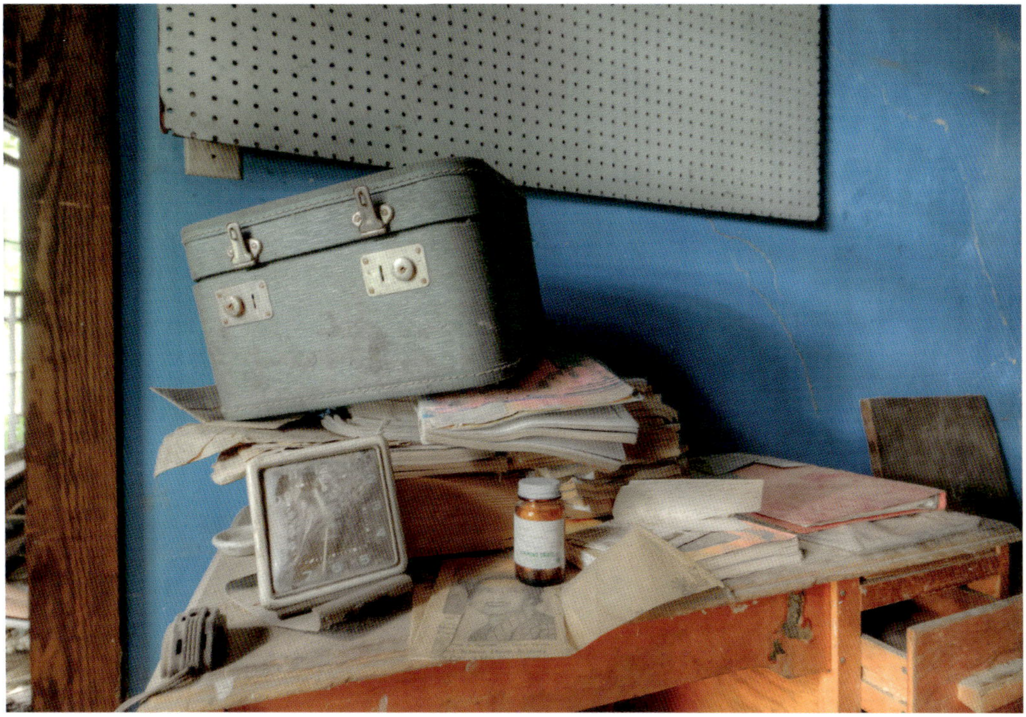

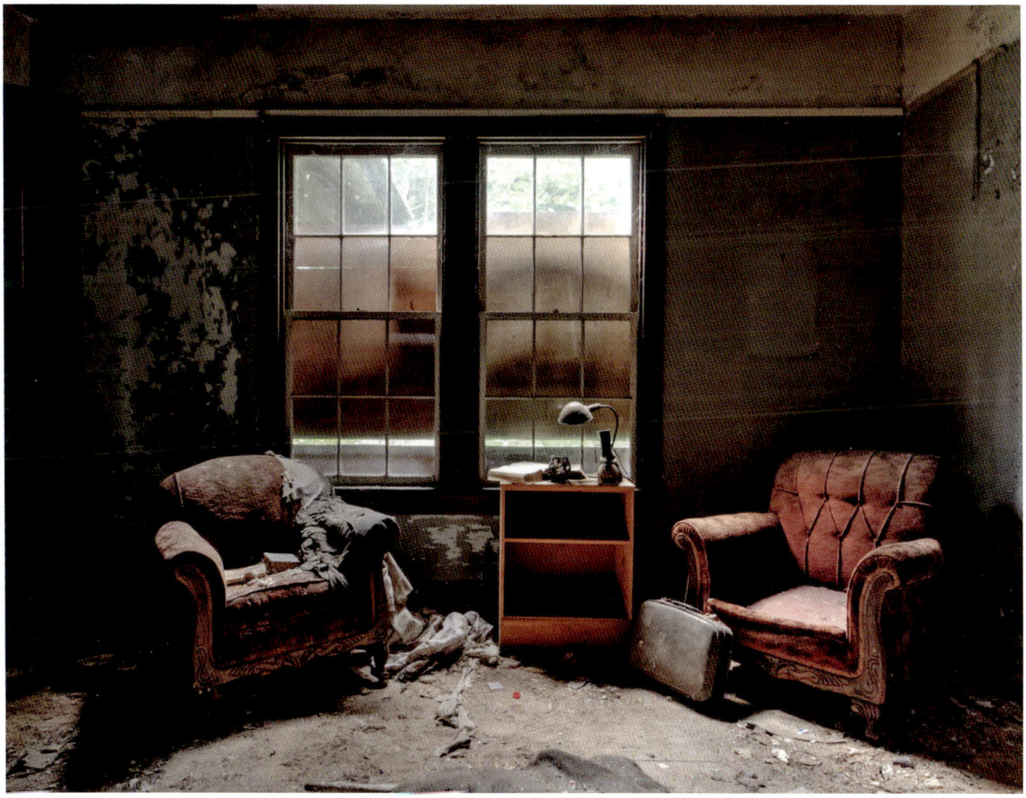

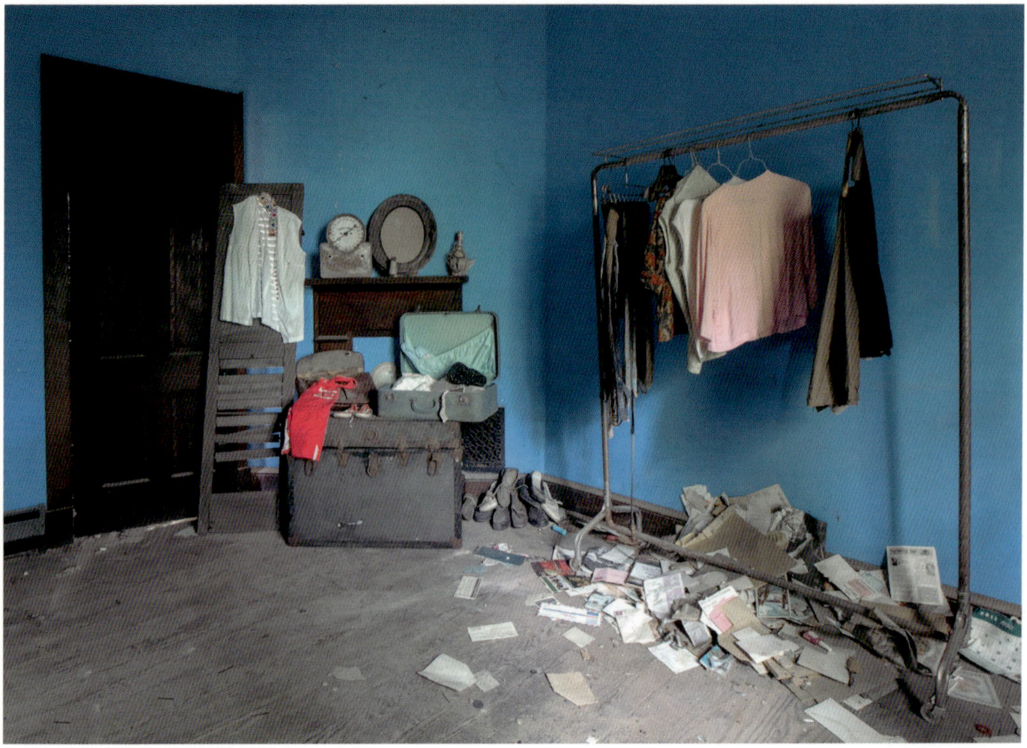

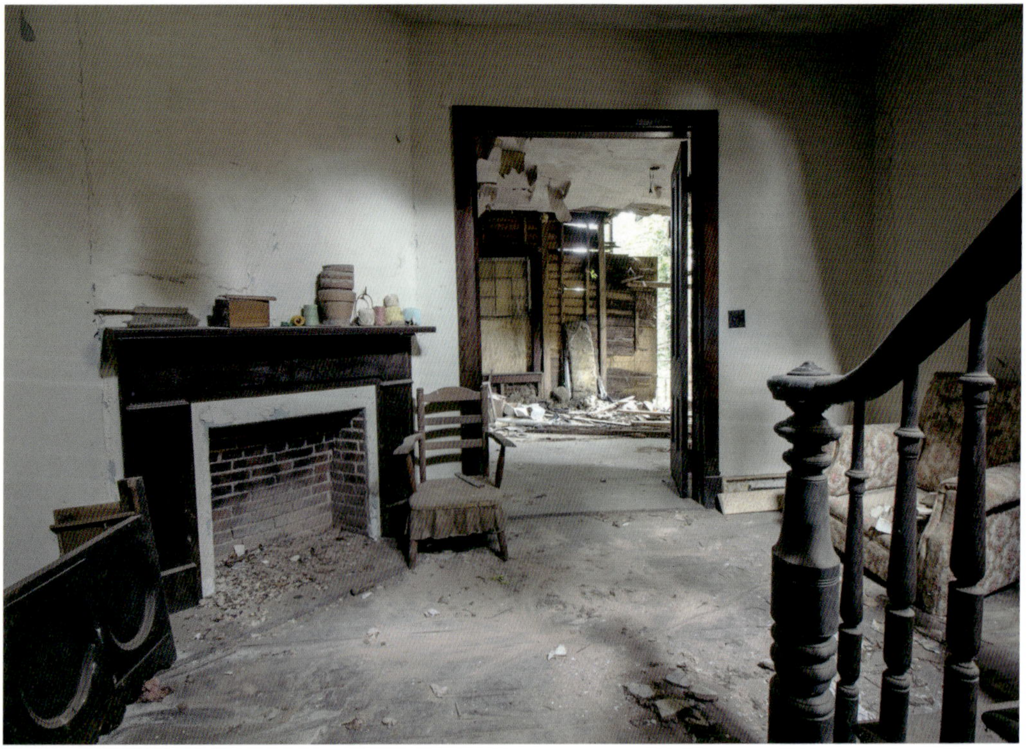

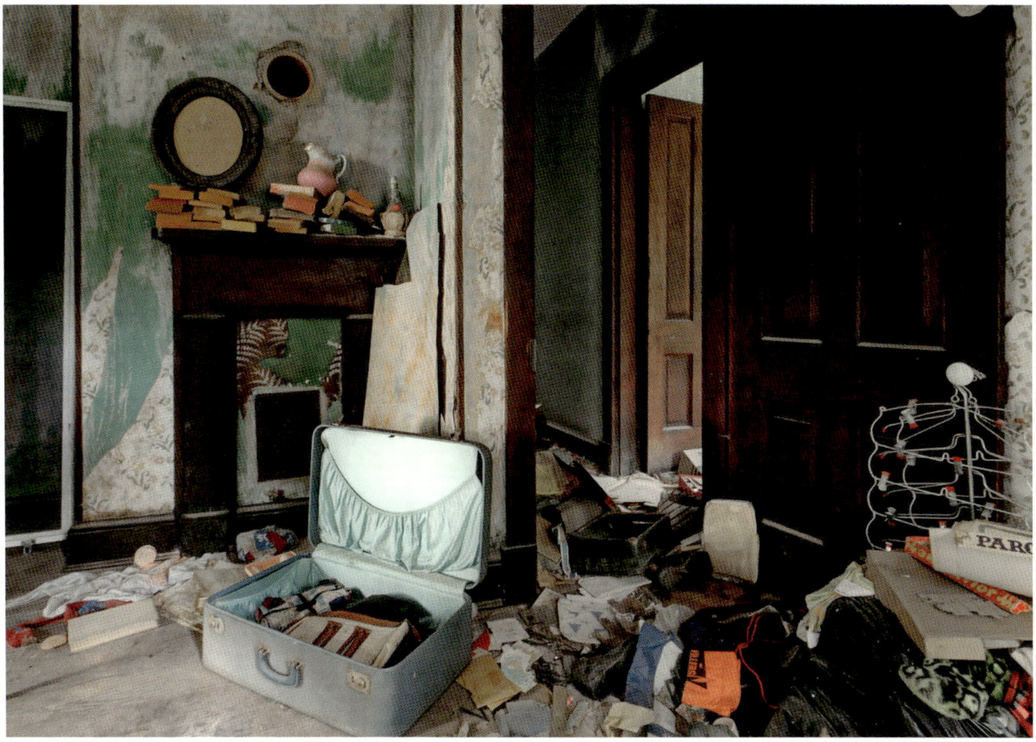

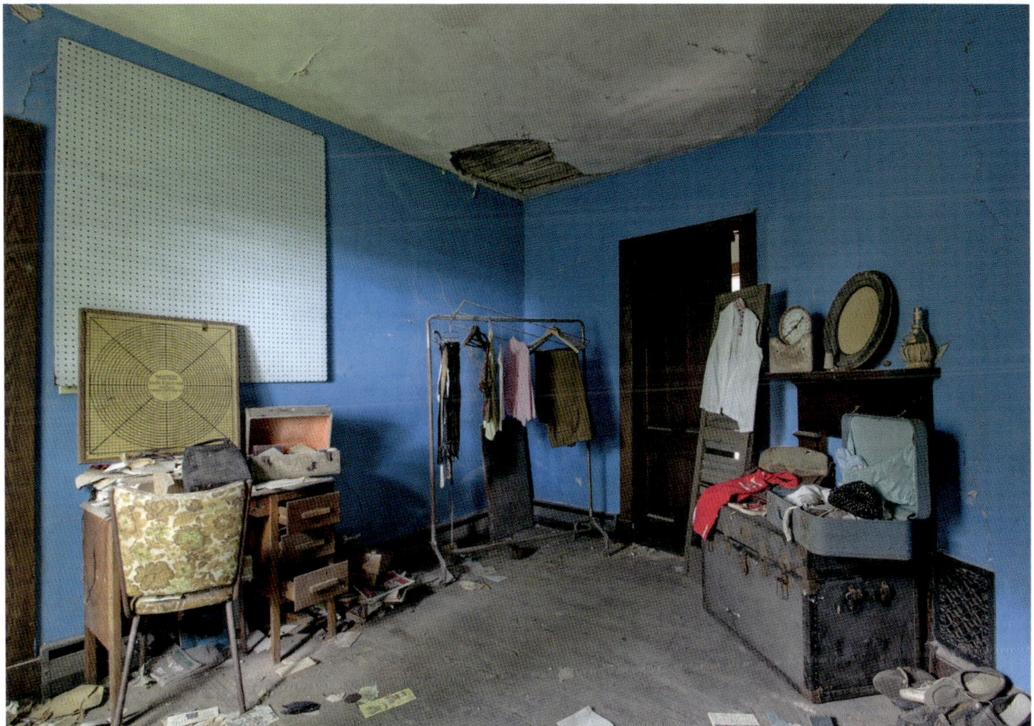

6

UPLANDS MANSION

When walking through this eerie mansion encased by an overgrown garden, Robyn felt the sensation that someone was watching us, and we were not welcomed. Renowned Baltimore socialite and philanthropist Mary Frick Garrett Jacobs once called this neglected forty-two-room Victorian home. Mary's father was a wealthy attorney, and her mother was a descendent of a former governor of Virginia, who had been knighted by James VI. The Uplands mansion property was owned formerly by her great-grandfather, John Swan, a Revolutionary War general and friend of George Washington. Her father presented the couple the mansion as a wedding gift. The manor was once part of Swan's larger Hunting Ridge estate. Before 1918, the Uplands area was part of Catonsville.

Mary Frick's husband, Robert, worked at his family's banking firm Robert Garrett and Sons before he succeeded the defeated Confederate General Robert E. Lee as president of the Virginia Valley Railroad. Robert incorporated Valley Railroad into B&O Railroad where his father John W. Garrett was president. After his father died, he became the president of B&O Railroad but resigned three years later in 1887. As a wedding present, John W. Garrett had gifted his son, Robert, and his bride, Mary, a lavish estate in Mount Vernon Place.

Mary and Robert resided at their house on Mount Vernon Place between November and Easter and returned to Uplands every spring; and in 1885, B&O architect E. Francis Baldwin renovated the property. Robert suffered from poor health for many years and died from kidney failure in 1896. Six years later, Mary married Garrett's close friend, his personal doctor, Henry Barton Jacobs. Mary would live off and on at the estate until she died in 1936, leaving the estate to the Episcopal Church and her vast art collection to the Baltimore Museum of Art. It took a while for the church to establish a use; but from 1952 to 1986, the mansion served as the Uplands Home for Church Women. Then, in the early 1990s, the New Psalmist Baptist Church bought the property and incorporated the historic building into its new church. After the New Psalmist congregation relocated, its building sat abandoned next to the desolate mansion. The church has been demolished. The house, now boarded and scarred with graffiti and trash, is an anachronism amid the recently developed Uplands townhouse community. Despite the vandalism, you can see elements of the mansion's once ornate architectural elements. As for not feeling welcome, Robyn felt it even more in an upper staircase to the final bedrooms. It gave her a chill on the back of her neck; it was as if an energy was telling her, "Get out."

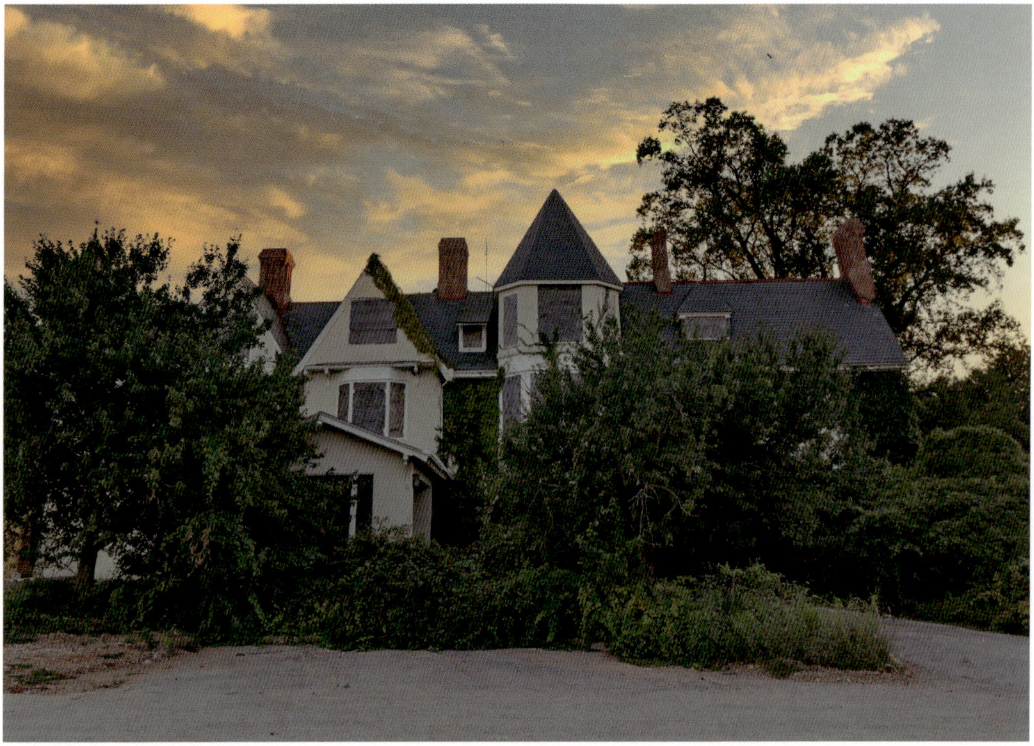

The sun sets on Uplands Mansion outside of Baltimore. [*Rhea*].

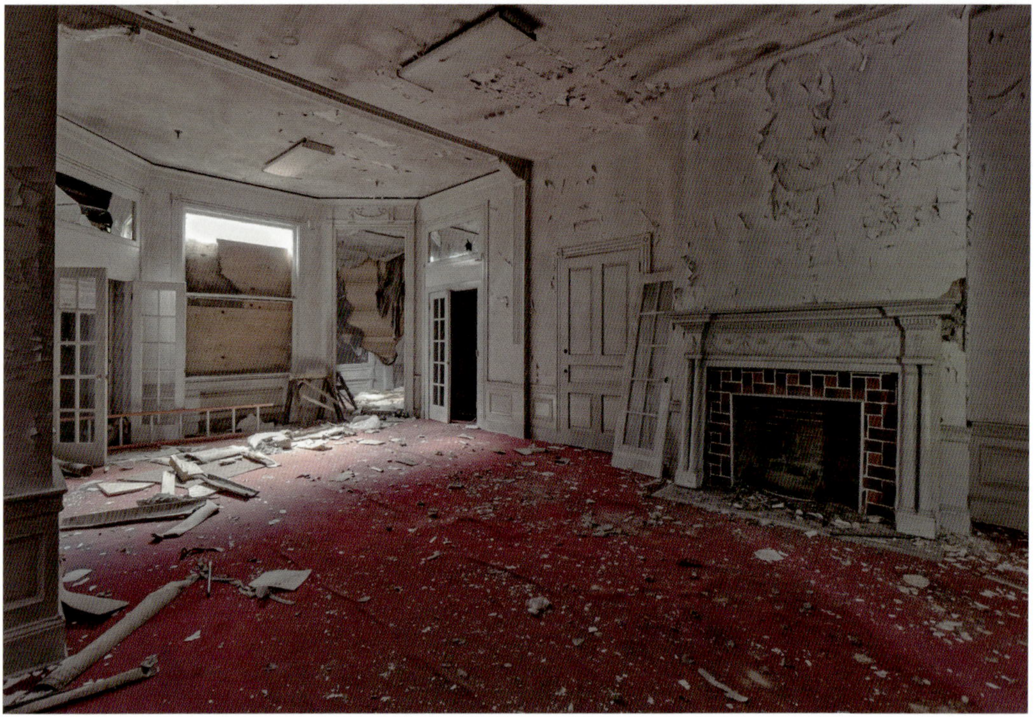

The front parlor of the Uplands Mansion is nothing more than gutted bones. [*Rhea*]

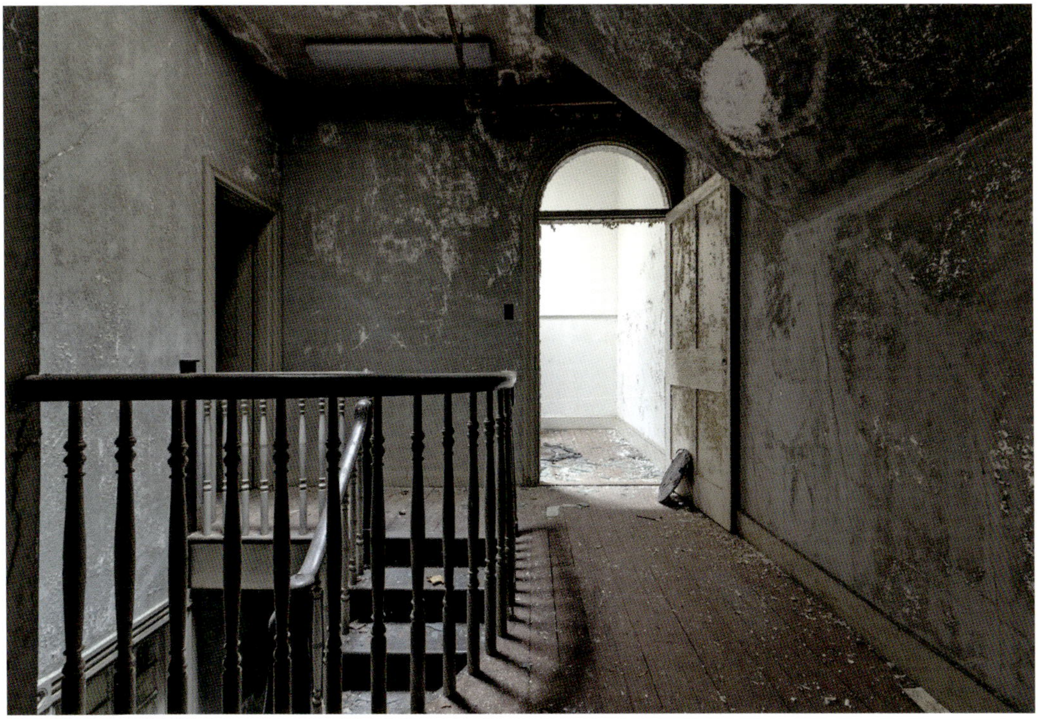

Robyn felt a supernatural presence around the creepy landing that leads to the final floors of Uplands Mansion. [*Rhea*]

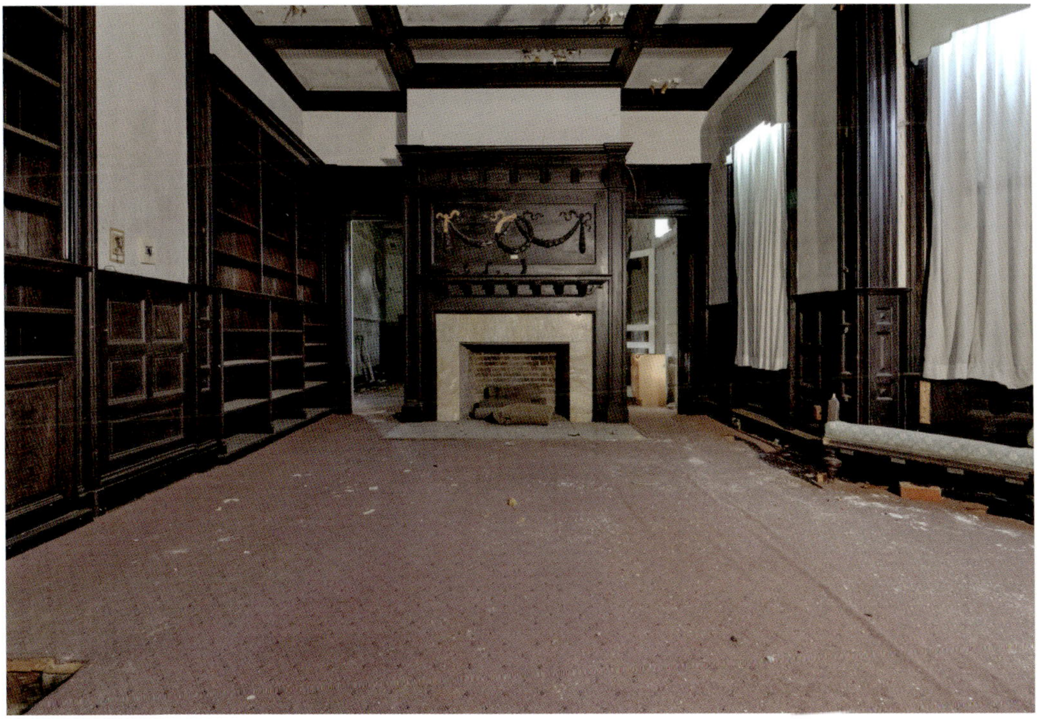

There is not much left of the mansion's library [*Rhea*]

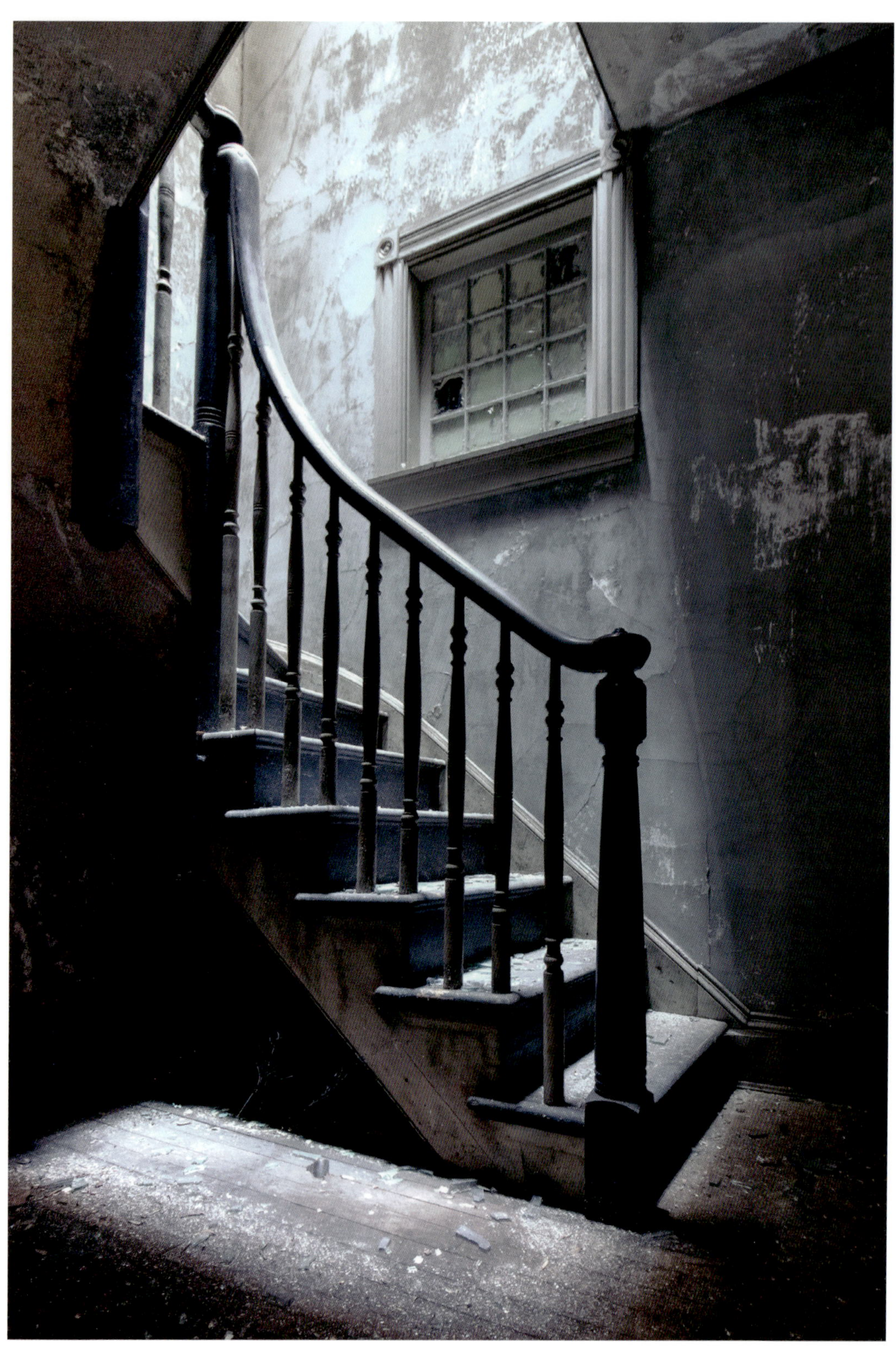

Servants' stairs in Uplands Mansion. [*Rhea*]

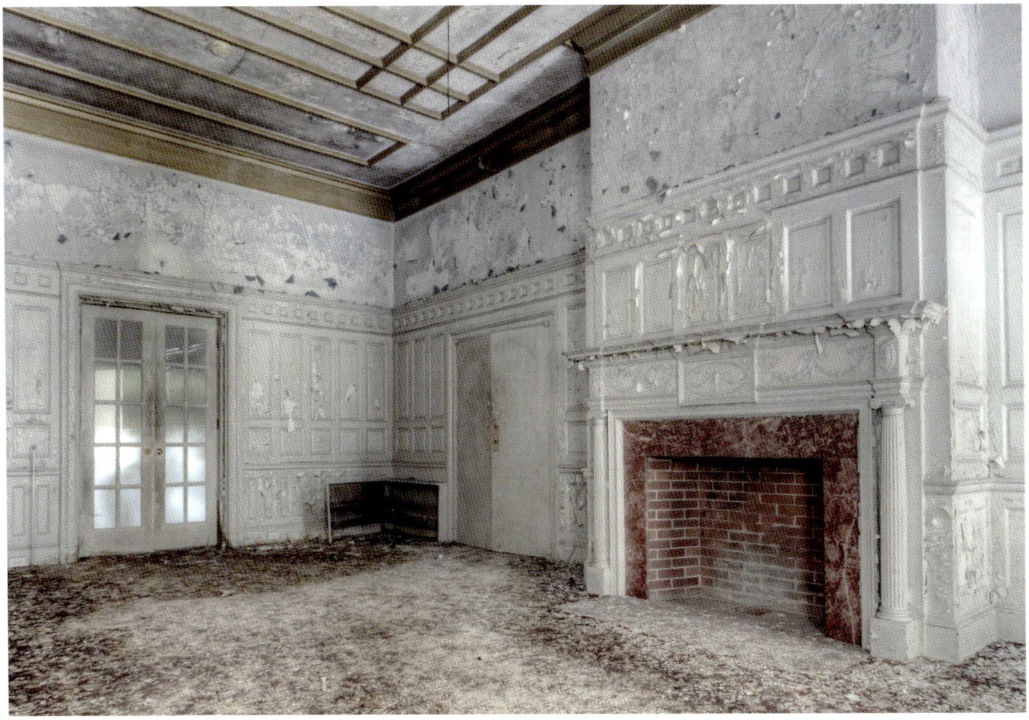

Another room left gutted inside Uplands Mansion. [*Rhea*]

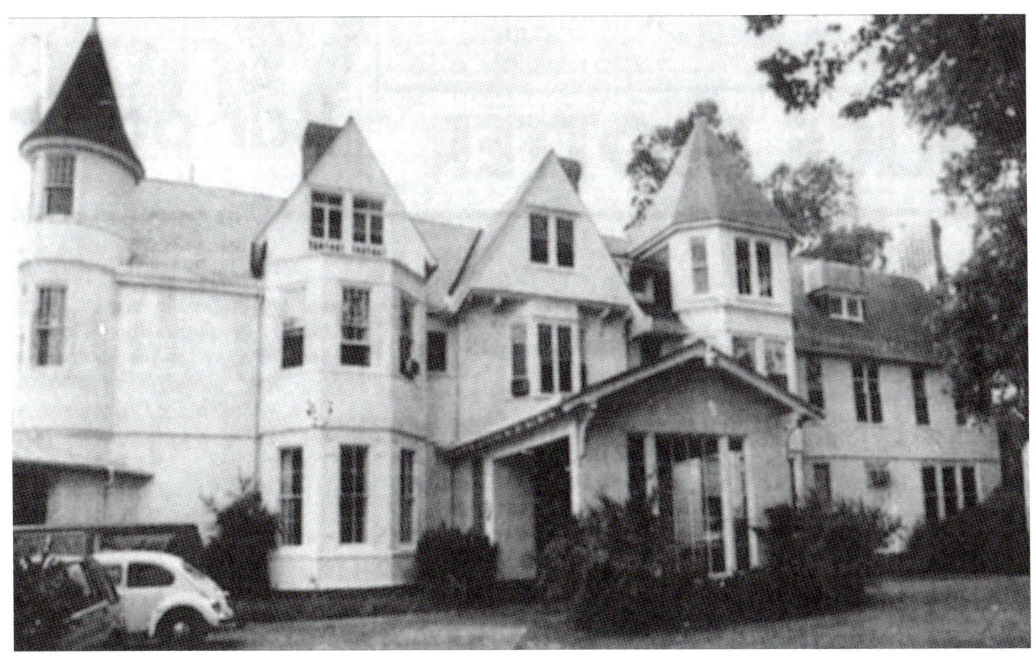

A historic photo of Uplands Mansion from the Enoch Pratt Free Public Library.

7

BALTIMORE AND THE ATHOL MANSION/ GUNDRY-GLASS SANITARIUM

If any mansion that we have explored was haunted by the supernatural, one would imagine it was the Second Empire mansion named Athol that once overlooked Southwest Baltimore. However, we actually felt no strange presence while inside, just a sense of melancholy and neglect. Amid trash and vandalism, it challenged our imagination to think of the mansion's original state. Athol began its days as the home for banker and Farmers Bank President Charles J. Baker somewhere between 1862–1864, according to the Maryland Historical Trust. When Baker died, the mansion sat in trust until 1900 when Dr. Alfred T. Gundry and his sister Edith E. Gundry bought it to create Gundry Sanitarium, a private sanitarium "for care of nervous disorders of women that required treatment and rest away from home." The grounds offered tennis courts, a bowling alley, greenhouse, gardens, and a gazebo. Alfred's father, Richard Gundry, was the medical director of Spring Grove, which was founded in 1797 and is the second oldest psychiatric hospital in the United States.

However, when Alfred's daughter died in 1986, the facility then was used as a mental health center for children at the direction of psychiatrist Dr. Sheldon Glass, but it closed in 1997 due to financial problems. Sheppard Pratt Health, an investor group, purchased it, followed by New Psalmist Baptist Church, and then the city of Baltimore. For nearly thirty years, the once lavish home sat vacant, filling with rubbish and falling prey to vandals until September 2021, when someone burned it to the ground.

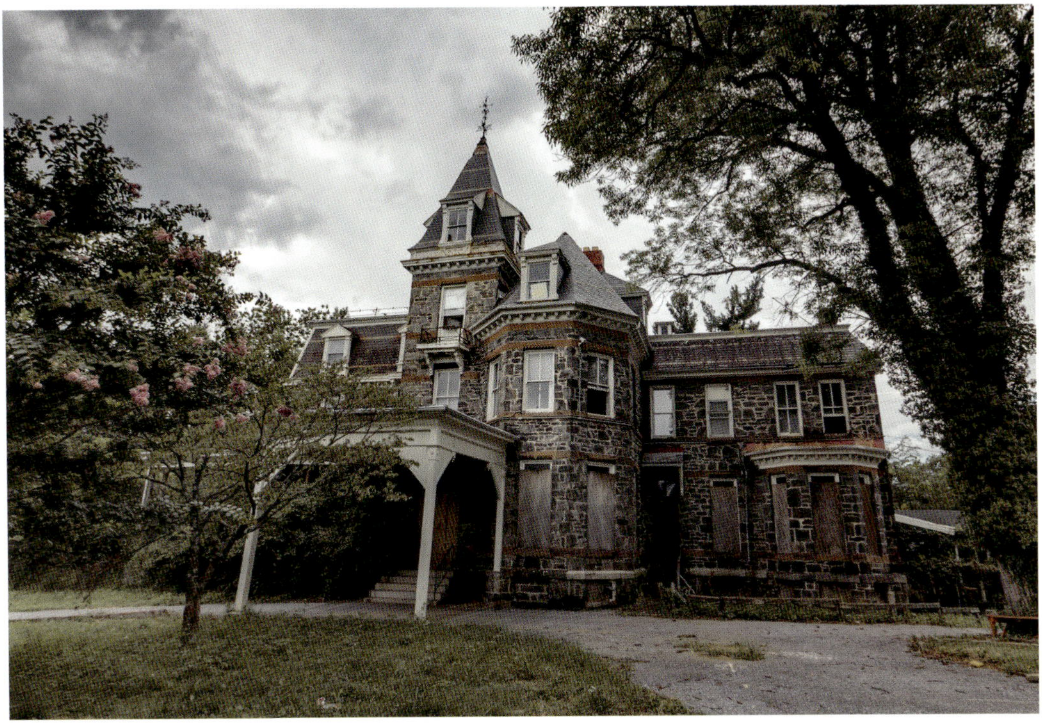

Originally built in the mid-1800s as a mansion for a prominent banker and glass maker, this Second Empire home evolved into a lavish, private sanitorium for women suffering with "nervous" and "mental disease." [*Rhea*]

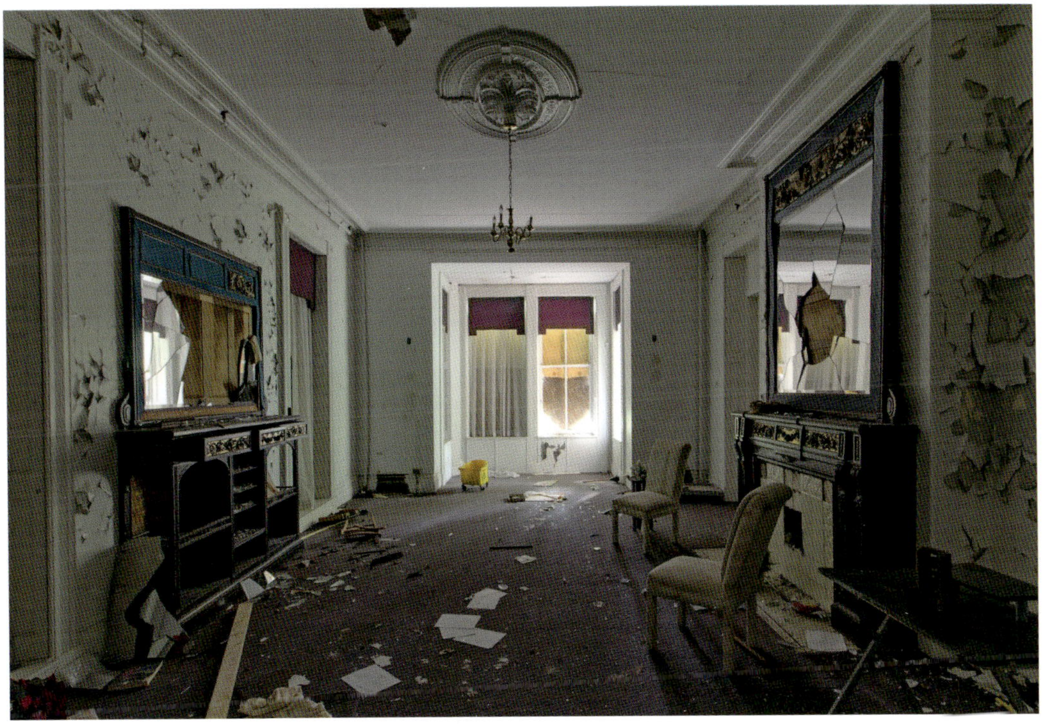

The sanitorium's parlor has been heavily vandalized. [*Rhea*]

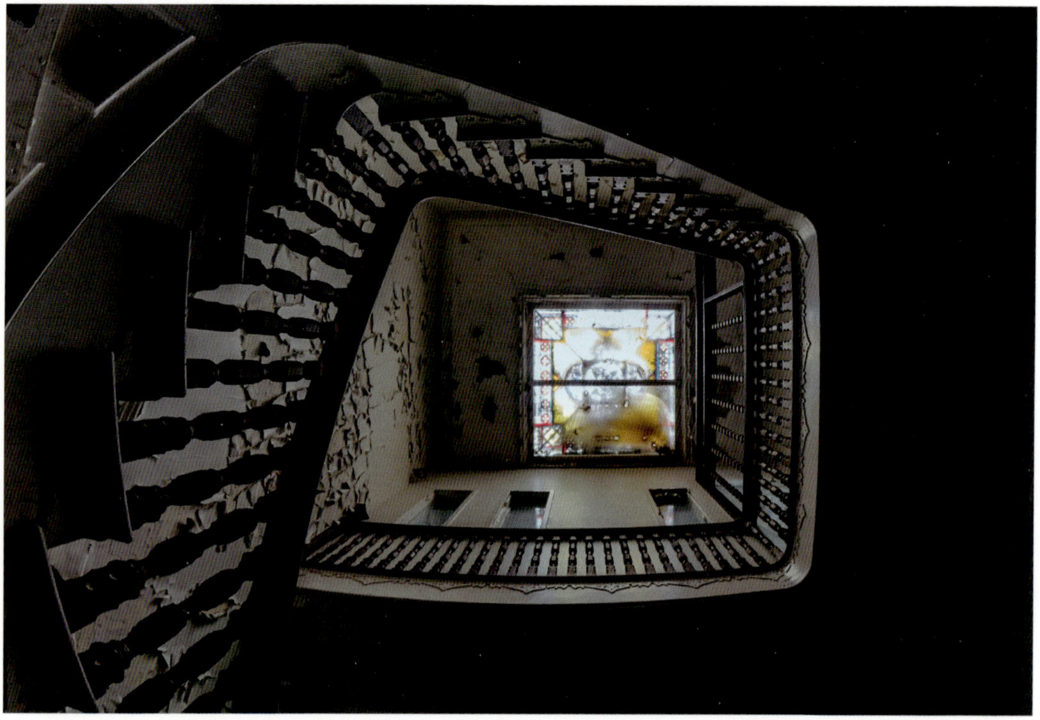

The sanitorium's spiral staircase leads to a stained-glass skylight. [*Rhea*]

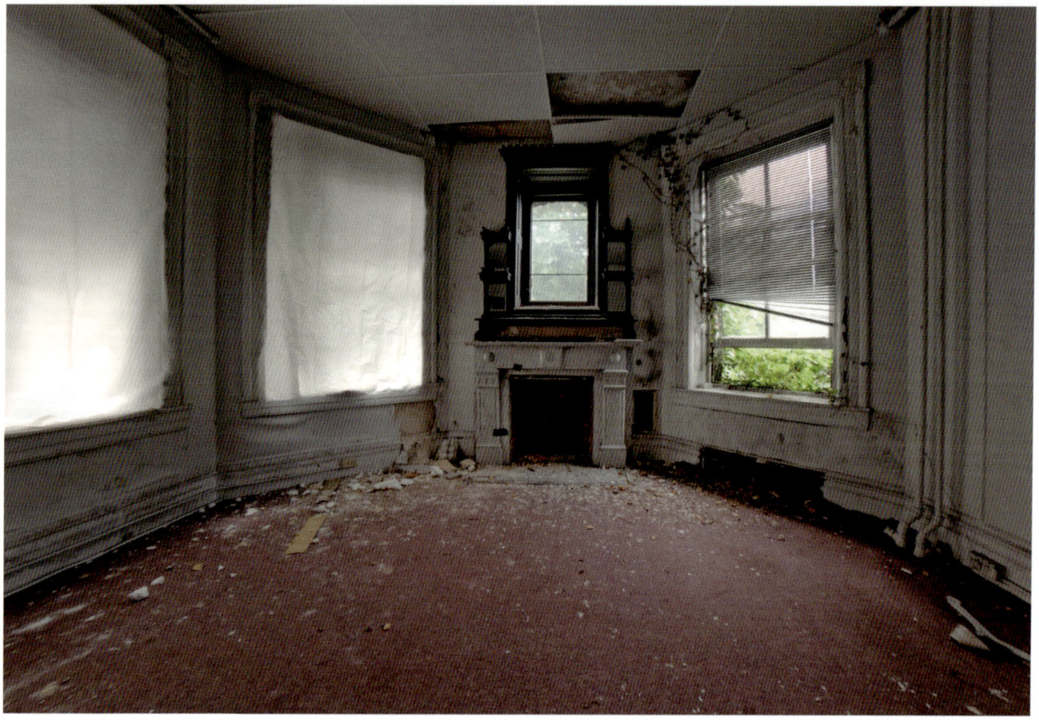

This is a fireplace inside an upstairs bedroom of the sanitorium's main building. The owners had expanded the hospital by adding cottages. [*Rhea*]

8

BLIGHTED BALTIMORE

We would be remiss if we did not include a few photos of the inner-city blight that plagues downtown Baltimore. These photos barely scratch the surface of the living conditions. According to online sources, Baltimore possesses more than 16,000 abandoned buildings. City officials have enacted legislation to demolish blight and to clean up the city. An explorer friend of ours from Canada said as we drove through the city, “This is America? This is a third-world country. How does the government allow people to live like this?” Many people are living in homes that appear as if they should be abandoned. The question lingers: How did the city evolve into a wasteland?

Its beginnings showed such promise as the Port of Baltimore served as an entry for commerce for 300 years, even connecting cargo with the B&O Railroad. Next to New York City, Baltimore shined as a haven for opportunity, because jobs were plentiful as industries manufactured everything from sugar, spice, and steel, to umbrellas. However, as the city grew, developers pushed to expand outside the town’s limits, building bungalows and excluding blacks from the opportunity to buy into these new neighborhoods. n the 1930s, banks began redlining the black neighborhoods in Baltimore, enacting unfair loan practices, resulting in lower homeownership for black families. The city transformed again in the 1950s when white GI’s returned home from World War II and built homes in suburbs in surrounding counties, resulting in a massive population decline. Retail companies and industry fled along with this mostly white population, emboldened by the new highway system. As a result, once bustling brick factories fell silent. The highways themselves were constructed to separate black communities from white neighborhoods.

Among Baltimore’s thousands of abandoned row houses is the Italianate Second Empire style Sellers Mansion in downtown that was once home to the railroad tycoon Matthew Bacon Sellers Sr., the president of the Northern Central Railway. Built in 1868,

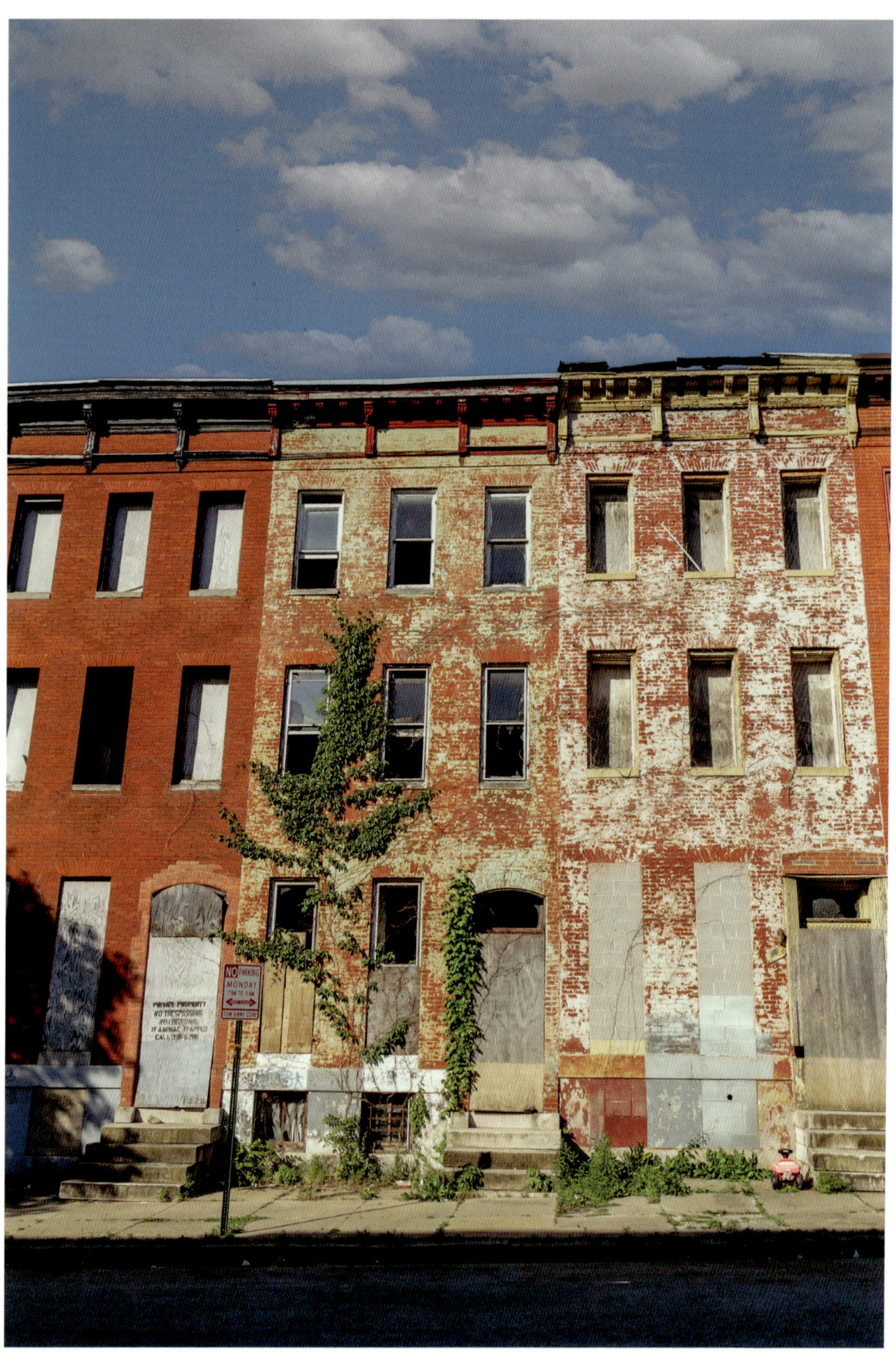

Baltimore possesses more than 10,000 abandoned buildings. [*Rhea*]

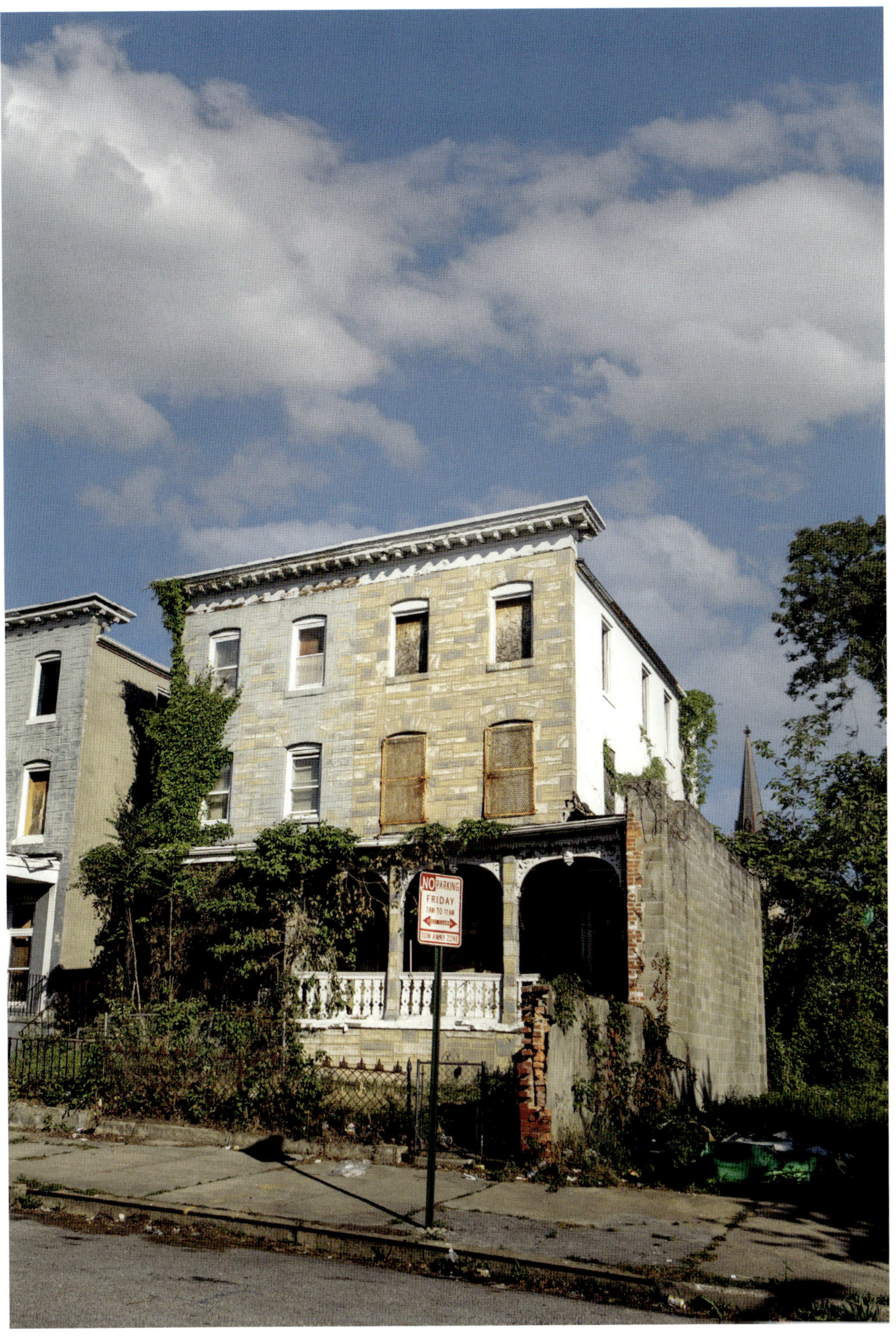
NO PARKING
FRIDAY
7AM TO 11AM
TOW AWAY ZONE

this National Register of Historic landmark is three stories high and was his country house and plantation. Nowadays, it is hard to imagine a country house existing in downtown Baltimore. The mansion contains a mansard roof, carved stone lintels, a patterned slate roof, and carved wood Corinthian columns. Sellers also owned a plantation in Louisiana.

Another abandoned relic of the city's wealth was constructed in 1838 for Baltimore lawyer David Stewart. Greek Revival Upton Mansion has sat abandoned in Baltimore for nearly twenty years. It used to sit on 10 acres and possess a grand porch with Doric columns. In the 1930s, one of the city's first radio stations took occupancy of the home, WCAO. The next owner was the Baltimore Institute of Musical Arts, which closed it after the desegregation of schools. The city school district then took ownership to create a center for special education, naming it Upton School for Trainable Children No. 303, according to Baltimore Heritage. The school district then housed its home and hospital services program in the mansion. The future plans for the mansion are to house an AFRO American Newspaper.

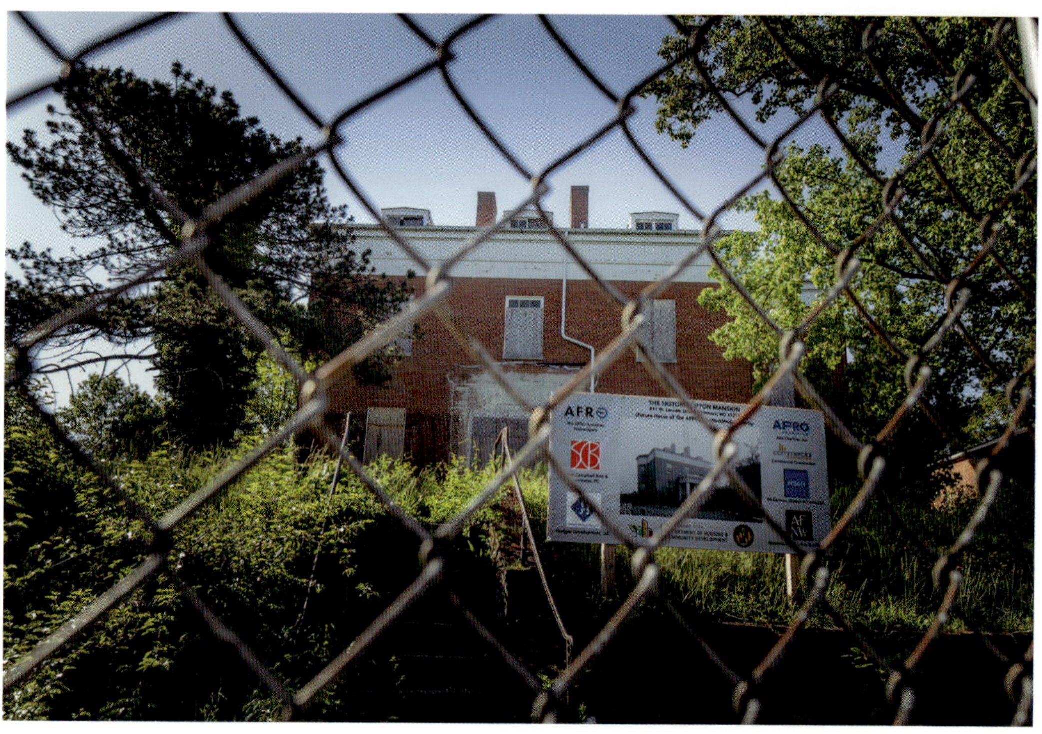

Constructed in the 1830s as a country house and plantation, the Greek Revival Upton Mansion has sat abandoned in Baltimore for nearly twenty years. Over the decades, the mansion has been home to many including a radio station and will soon house an AFRO American Newspaper. [*Rhea*]

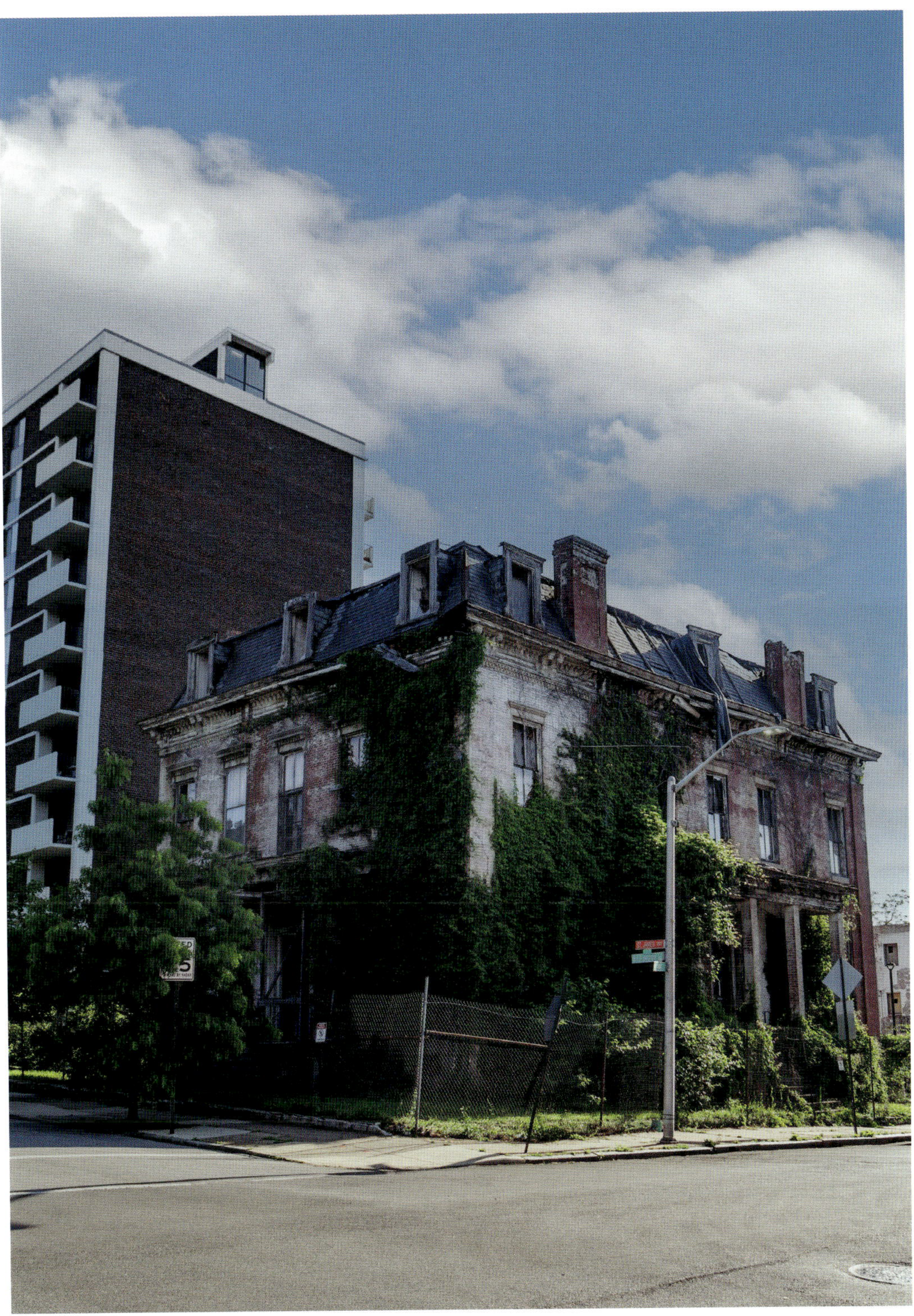

A side view of the long-abandoned Italianate Second Empire-style Sellers Mansion in downtown Baltimore. Built in 1868, this National Register of Historic landmark is three stories high and was built of brick for Matthew Bacon Sellers Sr., president of the Northern Central Railway. [*Rhea*]

FINAL NOTE

Since 2014, we have driven the backroads together, exploring the beauty of the Northeast and mid-Atlantic region. Along the way, we have strengthened our marriage while learning more about the history of those who came before us. We love exploring because it feels like we are walking in the past, as if we are archeologists of sorts. We want to remind you why we would not name or provide more details on all of the houses, because it is truly our wish to protect them from vandalism and theft. If you can, please consider donating at preservationmaryland.org/support. And, if you want to see more of our photography, you can find us on Instagram: @morning_reveries and @dorianhelix. Thank you for all your support.

Love,
Robyn and Rhea

REFERENCES

Baragona, S. "Rising Seas Forcing Changes on Maryland's Historic Eastern Shore," *Voice of America* (U.S. Agency for Global Media: October 29, 2018) voanews.com/a/climate-change-maryland-farms/4633200

"Charting the Multiple Meanings of Blight: A National Literature Review on Addressing the Community Impacts of Blighted Properties," The Vacant Properties Research Network (Virginia: Virginia Tech, 2015) kab.org/sites/default/files/ChartingtheMultipleMeaningsofBlight_FinalReport.pdf, 2015

"The History of Baltimore," *City of Baltimore Master Comprehensive Plan.* (Baltimore: City of Baltimore, n.d.) baltimorecity.gov/sites/default/files/5_History.pdf

"History of Maryland's Eastern Shore," *The Eastern Shore Guide* (Denton, MD: n.d.) easternshore.com/esguide/History

Kelly, J. "For Sale: The faded grandeur of the Winderbourne Mansion," *The Washington Post* (Nash Holdings, 2016) washingtonpost.com/local/for-sale-the-faded-grandeur-of-the-winderbourne-mansion/2016/04/18/2138eeda-0568-11e6-a12f-ea5aed7958dc_story

King, N. "A Brief History of How Racism Shaped Interstate Highways," *NPR* (PRI:, April 7, 2021) npr.org/2021/04/07/984784455/a-brief-history-of-how-racism-shaped-interstate-highways

"Maryland's History," The Secretary of State Kids Pages (State of Maryland: n.d.) sos.maryland.gov/mdkids/Pages/Maryland's-History.aspx

"Medicaid Issues in Probate Court How Medicaid Rules Impact Conservatorships and Decedents' Estates," (Alabama Legislative Services Agency, n.d.) lsa.state.al.us/PDF/ALI/judges_resources/2018_Summer_Conference/Medicaid.pdf

Meils, J. F. and Obando, S. "For Maryland's northern counties, the economic riddle is blending the old with the new," *Capital News Service* (University of Maryland: 2017) cnsmaryland.org/2017/06/02/for-marylands-northern-counties-the-economic-riddle-is-blending-the-old-with-the-new/

"The Other Maryland Farm Loss Factor: Salt Water Intrusion," (Montgomery Countryside Alliance, 2021) mocoalliance.org/news/the-other-maryland-farm-loss-factor-salt-water-intrusion

Russell, J., "Yaocomicos Help Calverts Settle in St. Mary's City," *The Lexington Park Leader*. (September 4, 2018) lexleader.net/yaocomicos-help-calverts-settle-in-st-marys-city/

"Stone Wall Field, (Enfield)," Maryland Historical Trust (State of Maryland: n.d.) mht.maryland.gov/secure/medusa/PDF/BaltimoreCounty/BA-2284.pdf

"Uplands," *Explore Baltimore Heritage*, explore.baltimoreheritage.org/items/show/311

Watters, S, "Visualizing Farm Loss," *Maryland Today* (University of Maryland: 2018) today.umd.edu/visualizing-farm-loss-6a296c40-4e00-4927-bdbf-607570d03ad1

"Why does Baltimore have so many vacant buildings?" (Baltimore Heritage, n.d.) baltimoreheritage.github.io/vacant-buildings-101/guides/history